A WALK IN HER SHOES

One Man's Journey into Feminism

TRAVIS GREENLEY

A Walk in Her Shoes: One Man's Journey into Feminism

Travis Greenley
63 Benjamin Cresent
Orangeville ON L9W 5J3
travisjg@hotmail.ca

Ordering Information:

Quantity sales. Special discounts are available on quantity purchases by corporations, associations, and others. For details, contact the publisher at the address above.

Cover designer: LeTeisha Newton; Beyond DEF
Editor: Tiffany Fox; Beyond DEF
Interior Layout: Deena Rae Schoenfeldt; E-Book Builders for Beyond DEF

Print ISBN: 978-19992619-0-0

Printed in Canada by Safeguard Business Resources

A WALK IN HER SHOES

One Man's Journey Into Feminism

"Are you a feminist?"

That is the question Travis Greenley has tried to answer for the last ten years. Working in an all-female environment in the field of violence against women has given Travis the chance to see things differently. But has that been enough to allow him to be called a feminist?

During his journey as a Violence Prevention Educator in local schools, Travis has tried to share what he has learned to help people explore the issues surrounding gender-based violence. From dads groups, to boys programs, and all the way to all-girls health classes, Travis has heard so many different life experiences. He has witnessed heartbreaking stories, hilarious moments, and courage that can help shape the next generation. Join Travis on his journey as he shares the highs and lows of working with children, learning about feminism, and ultimately finding his place in helping end violence against women.

Dedicated to Sabina and Katie.
You have shown me who I am and who I'm capable of becoming.

Together we can create change!

"We cannot all succeed when half of us are held back."

—Malala Yousafzai

INTRODUCTION

Trying to look somewhat dignified, I half walked, half stumbled along the road. I was determined to finish. I was determined not to fail. For some bizarre reason, my mind kept drifting to those annoying workout videos that always chanted, "Feel the burn." In that moment, I *was* feeling the burn, but unlike the videos, I wasn't finding it the least bit inspirational."

Out of the corner of my eye, I caught glimpses of familiar faces. I also heard faint sounds from all directions—some friendly, some mocking—and I think I even heard some whistles. I pulled my attention back to what I was doing and told myself, "Just put one foot in front of the other." The problem was that it seemed so far to go, and it felt like I was getting nowhere fast. How long could I last? Would I be the only one not to finish? No, that couldn't be how it ended. I had already seen some other people stumble and stop, so I had to be doing pretty well. However, the term "pretty well" could only refer to the fact I was still standing. Physically, I felt very far from "well." Perhaps I should have listened to the people who had suggested I take this more seriously.

"It's going to be tougher than you think."

"If you don't take this seriously, you'll regret it."

"You'd hate to get out there and look foolish."

"Maybe you should just do a few trial runs before the real thing."

Of course, I laughed at all those comments. How hard could it really be? I was in decent shape. I was still an active guy. I played sports, hiked regularly, and had recently taken up kayaking. I thought this would be a fun little event I could show up for and breeze through. Those thoughts seemed ridiculous now. If I had the strength and coordination left, I'd kick myself for my hubris and naïveté. But kicking was out of the question. Currently, walking was a Herculean task. The pain was increasing with each step. I began to ask myself how people did this regularly. I also asked myself *why* people did this regularly. I felt one leg weaken, and I stumbled, momentarily wondering if this was it. I regained my balance and corrected my movements before mentally scolding myself for allowing my mind to wander.

"Come on, you've come this far. Don't lose it now."

Back to basics; left, then right, and repeat. If I could keep it up for a little longer, I would be finished. Images began to flicker through my mind like one of those old-fashioned slideshows. They were of the people I was doing this for. I was determined to get this done for them.

It was as those images flashed before my eyes that I started to feel it; I was entering the home stretch. I heard the roar of the crowd even before the finish line came into focus. What seemed liked hours was now coming to a close. As people saw me approach the end, they probably thought I looked like a toddler taking his first steps—unsteady and unsure—but I didn't care. After all, you don't earn style points in something like this. It's all about endurance, will, and commitment, and right now, I had all those things.

Some people say when a boxer is being beaten and is about to go down for the count, they hear a voice in their head telling them to keep going. Some people say the boxer will find an inner strength when they have only one round left and suddenly become energized again. In those final moments, that was me. I had found that zone. I had found that final push allowing me to complete this arduous task. Just a few more steps and I would be there; nothing could stop me now. I forced myself to ignore the blister developing on my left foot. After all, nothing significant is accomplished without a struggle—this was my struggle. Then, it finally happened. I crossed the line that signified the end of this painful journey. I looked around and saw the smiling faces of the other participants.

We did it—*I* did it! Yes, there were times when I didn't think I could, and I'm sure that was true for all of the others as well, but we did it! We had finished. Each of us had just walked 100 yards in women's high-heeled shoes.

Mine were pink, size 10, and man, were they uncomfortable.

CHAPTER ONE
In Her Shoes

"Could a greater miracle take place than for us to look through each other's eyes for an instant?"

—Henry David Thoreau

Why walk in women's shoes? I can tell you it wasn't to strengthen my calf muscles. Although, come to think of it, my legs could have become extremely well-defined with a few more strolls in my pink stilettos. No, the real reason was empathy.

Empathy has long been described as "putting yourself in someone else's shoes and trying to understand their feelings and perspective." So that's what the group of men walking had tried to do that day in June when we took the 100-yard journey in our heels. Yes, it's true we did take the definition quite literally by actually wearing the shoes, but as I have learned, that's not completely unusual.

I had learned that fact a few years earlier when I had been assigned the task of teaching empathy to a group of seven-year-olds.

Now, you might think men and seven-year-olds understand things differently. However, in my experience, that's not always the case. When I taught empathy to that group of impressionable youngsters, I used that common phrase of "putting yourself in someone else's shoes." I watched their little faces as I described empathy, and I could actually see the information sinking into their young, malleable minds. I knew in that moment I had just taught them a valuable life lesson. In short, I had hit a home run!

Well, as many teachers will tell you, glory is often short-lived in the classroom. That was certainly the case on this occasion because, as I was confidently striding out of the classroom at the end of the day, I noticed a commotion at the coat racks. Before I knew it, several students were—yep, you guessed it—exchanging shoes. I will never forget the one little girl who looked up at me as she tried to cram her feet into a pair of sneakers that seemed far too small for her. Her face was so earnest and sincere as she said, "I know exactly how he feels. His shoes are really uncomfortable."

So, yes, we high-heeled walkers did take the definition of empathy as literally as a group of seven-year-olds, but we did it with purpose (and style if you saw us strut). In actuality, the walk was designed to bring attention to the issue of violence against women (VAW). Even more than that, the true purpose was to engage men in conversations about how they can play a role in addressing this important issue. Over 100 men walked, limped, or crawled across the finish line that day.

What most of them didn't know was that I had started my own journey in a woman's shoes over a decade earlier on December 16th, 2006. I didn't really understand I was doing that at the time though. I thought I was simply starting a new job. In reality, I was tentatively starting a walk into the world of feminism, violence against women, and a better understanding of our world.

When I first interviewed for my new job at the VAW organization I now call home, my motivation was simple. I wanted a job where I could work some regular hours, see more of my family, and do something I felt was important. I was also scared out of my mind. I would be leaving a job in which I made more money, had more room for advancement, and where I knew exactly what I was doing. If I got this job, I would have less of the first thing, very little of the second, and none of the third. But even with all that being true, there was something pushing me toward this opportunity.

That "something" was my two-and-a-half-year-old daughter Katie. Like most parents, having a child was life-changing for me. It meant less sleep, more stress, and a feeling of responsibility that felt like an anvil on my shoulders at times. But it also meant unconditional love, inspiration, and a new perspective on life. What was important before seemed less so now, and what were once the concerns of others suddenly became priorities for me.

The day I got my first push toward a new career and a life in feminism was a Friday. I was just about to leave for work. I would work ten hours that night, followed by two more ten-hour days. This would be the last time I'd see Katie until Monday morning. As I was getting ready for work that day, Katie asked me a simple and very innocent question most parents get asked at one point or another.

"Daddy, why do you have to go to work?"

"Daddy has to make money, sweetie," I replied without hesitation.

I didn't think much about my reasoning when I responded. I gave my wife and daughter a kiss and was out the door a few minutes later. As I pulled away, I could see my little family at the window waving goodbye. It was in that moment I rethought my answer to my daughter's question. Was that the message I wanted to send her? That you leave your family each day to make money? That money was my key motivation? We never know the moments that will send us down a new path, but that moment was mine. I wanted to have a better answer for my daughter. I wanted her to know me in a different way. I wanted my answer to be more like:

"What Daddy does is important. What Daddy does makes a difference."

That's what I wanted, so that's what I set out to find.

I was fortunate enough to find that position and began my new job on that fateful December day. My official job title was Violence Prevention Educator. The title has morphed over time into a few other incarnations (Youth Educator, Youth Education Facilitator), but the essence of the job has stayed the same. Explaining exactly what that job is to other people is sometimes an exercise in futility (Try floating the term Violence Prevention Educator at a party). I'm one of those people whose friends know where he works, but they really have no idea what he does. I've tried explaining it many different ways over the years.

Explanation: "I work for a women's shelter."

Response: "Oh, so you're a counselor."

Not exactly.

Explanation: "I work in the schools."

Response: "You're a teacher."

Not really.

Explanation: "I work to end violence in the community." (This was a real reach.)

Response: "I didn't know you were a cop."

I'm not.

To explain it as simply as possible, the agency I work for has a goal of eliminating violence against women. This is so fewer women and children will need to use their other services, including sheltering and counseling. Coming from a business background, I found this slightly bizarre at first. I equated it to McDonald's giving dietary counseling so fewer people would buy their products. However, as I quickly came to learn, the "business" of this organization wasn't only reserved for helping victims of violence, but its purpose was to also make sure people didn't become victims in the first place.

As a result, the agency I work for—which has had an emergency shelter and counseling services for decades to assist women who are leaving abusive relationships—decided to create a violence prevention program. The purpose is to educate school-aged children on the value of healthy relationships and all the related topics. The program deals with themes and topics like empathy, self-esteem, managing emotions, and understanding stereotypes. My job is to develop lessons and programs to engage the children in conversations and discussions that facilitate social and emotional learning. Ultimately, the objective is to stop violence before it happens and to put the other services out of business.

So with that important detail out of the way, we can move on to another important matter: the demographic make-up of my workplace. The day I started, I was the only male employee in an organization of almost forty staff members. Since that day, there have been two other male employees who have come through the doors, but I remain the only male who works there full-time. In short, I'm a man who works solely with women in the field of violence against women. It is a rare opportunity and gives me a unique perspective.

To be honest, I didn't completely understand this at first. The fact I was the only male working in an all-female environment got more attention from others than it did from me. Initially, I didn't really notice (I'm serious). When my students found out—especially the boys—they seemed to get really excited, as if I were the leader of some sort of harem. Even when I went to lunch with some of my co-workers, restaurant employees sometimes commented I was "taking my girls out to lunch."

But working in an all-female environment has been an extremely rewarding and eye-opening experience for me. First of all, there seems to be an abundance of the following things:

Meetings. Meetings about everything: who should clean up the client coffee station; how to improve inter-department communication (hint, the solution to the second topic was to plan more meetings); and there was even a meeting on how to plan for the next all-staff meeting.

Cake. There is cake for the obvious things like birthdays, baby showers, and going away parties. Then there is cake for meetings (of course), for someone doing well in their karate class, and I think we even had cake once because it was Thursday.

Compassion. The giving nature of my workplace and the remarkable women who work there opened my eyes to how much people are capable of giving to each other. Witnessing the daily acts of compassion and courage has made me a better person.

Feelings. This one really threw me at first. At the start of the many meetings, there is something called "check-in." This is a time reserved for talking about how you are and how you feel. The first time I witnessed this, I wondered what could possibly be happening. I mean, as a man from the business world, the only time I was asked about how I felt was when someone asked me how I felt about working an extra four hours, and they weren't really interested in my answer. But this was different. In this environment, they actually cared and wanted to know how people felt.

But I don't want to generalize and say that *all* predominately female working environments are like this because I'm sure they're not. Mine was and still is. It was something I found amusing and a little unsettling at first. But as time progressed, I couldn't imagine working in a place where these things didn't happen. So when people ask me, "What's it like to work with only women?" I don't hesitate when I say, "It's life-changing," because it has been. Not simply because of the three "C's" (communication, caring, and cake), but because of the different perspective it has offered me. It didn't take very long for me to realize this wasn't simply going to be a job but a life-defining experience that would challenge everything I thought I knew.

CHAPTER TWO
New Perspectives

"We are all here today because of the strength and courage of a woman. It's how we all enter this world."

1st Nations Introduction at a VAW Conference

"So … *are* you a feminist?"

I stared at this angry-looking woman with wild hair, a loud sweater, and crossed arms as she waited for my reply. It was my first month on the job, and logically, my program manager thought it would a good idea for me to receive some training. It was a one-day conference held annually by a provincial organization of which my agency was a member. It was held in a larger city about an hour from home and had staff members in attendance from many different women's shelters across Ontario. I was warned on the drive down by some of my co-workers that I might receive some looks or questions when I arrived. At that time, there weren't many organizations in the VAW sector that had male staff members, so I would probably stand out as a bit of an oddity. They also kept warning me specifically about a woman named Phyllis. They said things like:

"If you get cornered by Phyllis, one of us will come rescue you."

"Don't worry, Phyllis may just try to test you to see what you're all about."

"Her bark is worse than her bite. Just be yourself and you should be fine."

I wasn't nervous or worried before, but I was starting to feel a little uneasy now. As it turned out, this was the first time I truly took a walk in a woman's shoes. And to be honest, there are still some nights I wake up screaming about it.

I entered the large conference room where there were well over 300 people in attendance. This means there were well over 300 *women* in attendance. As I mentioned before, the fact I was the only male working in my organization rarely ever seemed relevant to me. But here, that seemed like the most relevant thing of all. I looked around and felt the regular kind of awkwardness many people feel when they enter a room where everyone else seems to know each other. That awkwardness soon changed to a very uncomfortable feeling of being watched. I suddenly felt very different, almost exposed.

At first, I tried to casually glance around the room to see if I could spot another male. After a little while, I actively searched for another male. Feeling completely different from everyone else was the weirdest thing. I had never experienced being in the minority. After all, I had been a white male who worked in business in a relatively small town. You can receive all the training you want. You can talk for hours about different issues people experience in our world. But nothing will allow you to understand a new perspective like living it. I had been living it for about six minutes and already understood the feeling of being a minority. I imagined this is what a person of color experienced in my hometown, or how a woman might feel in an all-male work environment. No one was intentionally trying to make me uncomfortable; they were just going about their business as usual. That is, everyone except for Phyllis.

As I scanned the room looking for a friendly place to settle, I noticed a woman staring at me. We locked eyes for a moment, and before I knew it, she was on the move. She advanced toward me with an obvious sense of purpose that left me with no other conclusion than I had done something wrong. I quickly looked to my left and then to my right to see if one of my co-workers was close by, but no one was. I felt like I was on an island all by myself, except for the angry-looking visitor rapidly approaching.

"So … *are* you a feminist?"

I was more than a little taken aback. I didn't know who this person was, why she was so angry at me, or most importantly, if I was a feminist or not. Something clicked in my brain as I stood there looking a little dumbfounded. Sadly, what entered my mind was not the answer to the important question that had been just posed to me, but rather, "This must be Phyllis!"

"Are you a feminist or not?"

That was the question. As I mentioned, when I entered this job just a month prior, the deep introspective questions and issues weren't my main priority. At that moment, it certainly felt like they should have been. I had heard the word "feminist" before. I knew in the vaguest of terms what it meant, but I wasn't sure how I was supposed to answer that question. Should I answer "yes?" But what if this woman felt a man couldn't be a feminist? I surely couldn't answer "no." I couldn't imagine that response putting a smile on her face. I decided to go with an approach that had worked for me in the past—honesty.

"If you're asking me if I believe men and women should be treated equally, then yes. I don't know if that makes me a feminist, but I do believe everyone should have the same rights."

I waited for her response. She seemed to be mulling over my answer. I didn't know how my answer sounded. Naïve, dismissive, offensive? God, I hoped not. I watched as her scowl slowly turned quizzical and then into a broad grin. Her shoulders dropped, and before I knew what was happening, she enveloped me in a large bear hug. She then clapped me on the back and said, "Hi, I'm Phyllis."

I didn't have the heart (or guts) to say, "Yeah, I know."

That was the day my perspective about my new job began to change. I left that conference with questions I had never considered before:

"*Was* I a feminist?"

"As a man, was I *permitted* to be a feminist?"

Of course, before I could answer either of those questions, there was the most important one:

"What *was* a feminist (really)?"

Historically, there have been many different waves of feminism, and it has taken many different forms. Essentially, feminism is the acceptance of a core set of beliefs:

- Women and men should have equal rights and opportunities.
- Women are intellectual and social equals to men and should be treated as such.
- Sexism exists.
- Sexism against women and misogyny is systemic, cultural, and ingrained.

It seemed pretty clear, straightforward, and logical to me. Of course, I believed in equal rights and opportunities. It was ridiculous to me that anyone *wouldn't* consider women equal to men in all aspects of life. That's how I was raised.

I grew up in a household where there were no jobs specifically for men or women. My dad did laundry and cooked just as much as my mom worked outside the home. I was taught respect was never based on one's gender and all people should be treated equally. So, when I compared my upbringing and views to the first two points of feminism, it seemed easy to conclude I was essentially a feminist.

Or was I?

Did I have the other core beliefs?

Did I believe or understand sexism and misogyny still existed and they were an ingrained part of our world?

To be honest, I had never really thought about it. As a young man, I never really *had* to think about it. But now, working in the VAW field and having a young daughter, it was something I was thinking about a lot. It was a question I would carry with me into my role as a youth educator in classrooms. It was there, in the classroom, the question would be answered for me very quickly.

CHAPTER THREE
Learning in High School

"You don't have to be anti-man to be pro-woman."

—Jane Galvin Lewis

"Hey, sir. Do you want to come outside with us and smoke a cannon?"

"I don't think my boss would like that too much."

"Don't worry. We won't tell on you."

This was one of the countless interactions I've had with high school students over the years. From my perspective, the best *and* worst thing about high school students is the honesty. They tell you what they think even if they think you're a complete idiot.

"Sir, can you come back to do this at two o'clock?"

"Why, is that a better time for the presentation?"

"Yes, sir … because we're done with school by then." (I really set them up for that one).

One thing I find amusing and interesting about high school students is their use of the words "Sir" and "Miss." They seem to think it will make everything else they say afterward sound more respectful. They will use the term when asking a question or when they are calling a teacher or guest the biggest moron they have ever known. But, without question, the greatest thing about high school interactions is they are always authentic; sometimes, they're more real than you are prepared for.

My initial foray into the classroom on behalf of my new job was in a high school. I was assigned the task of holding workshops for ninth- and tenth-grade students. My job was to ensure I visited every class in a local high school at some point during the month and conduct an interactive session about relationship violence and sexual assault. That meant *all* classes. There were history classes, science classes, math classes, and even a ninth-grade, all-female health class.

To be honest, the female health class was more than a little intimidating. Think about it: a middle-aged man talking to a group of fourteen- and fifteen-year-old girls about the difference between healthy and abusive dating relationships. Put yourself in their shoes. "What does this guy know about us or our lives?" At least, that was my thought going in. But, as is often the case, the students rose to the occasion and proved they were more open and accepting than any audience I could expect.

On this particular day, the lesson went extremely well. Yes, there were giggles and whispers as we moved on to some of the more sensitive subject matter. This included starting to navigate the slightly uncomfortable (for me) waters of sexual harassment and assault. The girls particularly enjoyed this part, especially when I explained sexual assault is about power and control and not about arousal. How did I know they enjoyed this part? They asked me to say the word "arousal" three more times.

"Oh my God, he said, 'arousal!' Sir, please say it again."

In summation, I survived the experience. Actually, that's not completely accurate. I thoroughly enjoyed the experience. Sure, I was a little uncomfortable, and I'm sure that was quite apparent at times, but I also really enjoyed the students' candor and openness in discussing such important matters. With that said, I was still looking forward to getting out of the classroom before I could embarrass myself more.

Before I could put on my coat, I noticed a group of four girls whispering to each other as everyone else filed out of the room. It was clear they wanted a moment of my time. I thought they only wanted to hear me say "arousal" again. But what they wanted was much more important. Slowly, the girls approached, and I heard one of them say, "You need to tell him."

The girls came closer, and I noticed one of them looked terrified and had tears welling in her eyes. She looked at the floor as she started speaking to me in a shaky, quiet voice.

"You know that stuff you talked about in class today? Well, it happened to me."

Part of me was terrified, but the other part was completely consumed by empathy and compassion for the pain this courageous young woman obviously felt.

"Do you want to tell me what happened to you?" I asked, wondering if that was the right thing to say.

"Well … I went to a party in the summertime, and a guy who was there raped me. I thought we were just messing around at first. But then he wouldn't let me leave, and it happened. I thought it was my fault, but then you said today that it wasn't. I don't know what to do."

This was all coming out in a sudden rush like a dam releasing a huge flow of water. She leaned against her friends like she was trying to stay upright as she told her story. Honestly, I didn't know what to do. No one had told me this might happen. I guess I was naïve to think you could talk about these sensitive issues and not have it trigger some personal stories, but that's exactly what I was. I was naïve to what women experience, and I was naïve to how often it occurred.

In that moment, I did what was natural—I listened. I told her it wasn't her fault, and I made sure she got the counseling she was going to need. In the end, it was a positive and important experience for that brave teenage student. It was also important for me, but it left me a bit shaken. It was the first time someone had ever confided in me that they had been a victim of violence. I say it was the first time because, sadly, it wasn't the last. Since then, I have spoken to church groups, service clubs, town and city councils, boards of directors, and classrooms, and it still stuns me a little when a woman or girl steps forward and shares her story. It doesn't happen every time, but it occurs far more often than not.

As I said, this first time left me more than a little shaken. It made me think about my little girl at home.

Something like what happened to that courageous teenager couldn't happen to my daughter, could it?

Was my daughter more likely to be a victim of violence simply because she was born a girl?

Was that possible in Canada?

All of this forced me to reflect on those remaining core beliefs of feminism:

- Sexism exists.
- Sexism against women and misogyny is systemic, cultural, and ingrained.

Statistics currently say that 51% of Canadian women experience some form of physical or sexual violence in their lifetime. That meant more than half the women I would meet in my life would experience violence committed against them. Just through meeting people in my new role, I was quickly learning this was absolutely true. This statistic, along with the personal stories I was exposed to, had forced me to take a hard look at the world in which I was raising my daughter.

It also made me truly think about the organization I was working for and the other services offered there. We had a shelter, and everyday of the year it was filled with women and their children who were leaving abusive relationships. We had a counseling program with a list of almost 100 women waiting to get support for the abuse they were facing.

All of this was happening in my hometown. I had grown up there, but I had never considered it to be a violent or dangerous place. That was the point. It wasn't violent or dangerous from my perspective, but it certainly was from many women's perspectives. It was that difference in perspective which had helped create the problem.

How can men be part of a solution when they don't fully understand the problem? Even more clearly, how can men be part of a solution to a problem they don't even know exists?

I began to think of it this way: what if an intersection in our town was so dangerous, people were injured or killed on a regular basis? How much attention would that problem get? How fast would the issue be addressed? I'd venture to say the community would be up in arms and the response from local decision makers and law enforcement officials would be swift.

But in our town, as in most towns, we *do* have a problem of women being injured on a regular basis. Sadly, some even lose their lives, yet few people know there is a problem. I was a perfect example of that.

Until I'd entered the VAW field and metaphorically began my journey in a woman's shoes, I had no idea violence against women was such a prevalent and destructive issue in Canadian culture. While I was starting to understand more about the issue, I still couldn't clearly make the connection between the heinous acts of violence I was hearing about and the core issues of feminism that included sexism and misogyny.

To understand the root cause, I would need additional time and more professional and personal self-discovery. Luckily, I had very strong women who were willing to teach me what I needed to learn—the women I worked with and the women I had in my life at home.

CHAPTER FOUR
Not These Balls!

"There's nothing more fun than entertaining kids."

—Jerry Seinfeld

I was living a life of self-discovery during my initial years in my new role, but there was still the day-to-day work that needed to be done. Not all of it was life-changing and full of deeper meaning. When you're working with children, sometimes it's just silly and fun. By the start of the next school year, the program I was a part of had begun to explode. We were quickly learning there was a significant demand for the type of information we provided. Administrators, teachers, and parents wanted their children to be exposed to messages of self-esteem, healthy relationships, and acceptance.

Schools were also seeing a difference in how their students were behaving at school after taking part in our programs. The students loved what we were doing in their classrooms, and it was having an impact on them. What the students seemed to enjoy most were the interactive and experiential components of the program. We decided very early on we wanted to make these heavy and sometimes very personal topics as fun and interactive as we could. Games, music, videos, drama, and even art were all integral parts of each lesson. As a result, we were overwhelmed with requests.

Most of these requests were coming from elementary schools. We had found our niche in fifth- to eighth-grade classrooms. These students were old enough to handle the topics but young enough that the schools believed behaviors could be significantly challenged and changed. With things so busy, there often wasn't a lot of time for self-reflection on what we were doing. It was easy to get caught up in the day-to-day life of working with kids. Yes, it was important and meaningful work, but sometimes it was simply fun.

I learned early in my work with younger students that they were used to rules. True, sometimes they don't follow them, but they certainly know they're there. When you try to explain to kids an activity has no rules, it quite often requires a more detailed explanation than if you were teaching them to play Monopoly for the first time. I learned this the hard way during that busy and frantic first full school year. It came into clear focus for me when trying to run a painting activity with a group of fifth-grade students.

"Okay, everyone, today we're going to paint our anger. There are no rules as to how it should look or what you have to paint. You can paint what makes you mad, what your anger looks like, or what you look like when you get angry."

Without fail, seventeen out of twenty students shot their hands in the air and began to pepper me with the following questions:

"What do we paint?"

"How big does it need to be?"

"What if you can't paint very well?"

"What colors do we need to use?"

I tried to calmly explain there were no rules in the art we were creating. They could paint whatever they wanted, and since it wasn't going to be evaluated, they didn't have to be artistic to do it well. At this point, a hush fell over the class. Obviously, I had explained the activity and myself well. Everyone seemed to be thinking. I assumed they were silently planning their artistic creations in their heads. I was just about to pass out the paper when one hand went up.

"But what do we paint?"

After several more explanations, we finally got underway. Once the students got going, it was amazing to see what they could create. There were pictures of tornados of anger, mad monsters, fires burning in bellies, and bottles trying to keep the anger inside. Of course, when working with a group of ten-year-old students, most of them want to share. It's not uncommon to see every hand in the class raised in response to a question or wanting to share a story. One of my favorite moments happened when a fifth-grade student responded.

"I have three things to share."

If you've ever worked with ten-year-olds, you realize each thing will take about ten minutes. You can imagine the time crunch when trying to give thirty ten-year-olds time to share their creations.

On this particular day, we had navigated the sometimes frustrating and always-messy minefield of creative painting, and we had moved on to the sharing phase of the lesson. Student after student came to the front after reaching as high they could with their hand to volunteer with the obligatory grunting sound of, "Oh, oh, pick me." Often, when a student arrived at the front of the room, it looked as if they were completely shocked they'd ended up in this position. Their face read something like, "Well, I can't believe I'm actually here—I wish I had more time to prepare for this."

The sharing was often similar from person to person, and the students seemed overwhelmed by this once-in-a-lifetime opportunity. But occasionally, we would get a special moment of sharing when everyone would learn something new. We would get a student who made such a meaningful connection, it would seem to bring focus and clarity to everyone's world. That was what we called the "aha" moments. This tale isn't about one of those moments, but it is about an equally memorable moment of sharing.

A boy named Max came to the front of the room, and as every kid before him, he had looked completely shocked he was being asked to speak publicly. I could see on his face a combination of wonder, amusement (that people were watching him), and fear. It only lasted for a few seconds before he seemed to gain his composure.

"Well, I get angry a lot," Max began.

I knew this from my experience in Max's classroom and from what his teacher had shared with me. The hope was this activity might give Max an outlet for his anger. Max stopped talking and looked around the room. The class seemed unsure if he was finished or if this was a prelude into an incredible presentation. Max took a deep breath, and his next sentence came out in one large rush.

"When I get angry, I paint balls."

Everything was silent. Max had a completely satisfied look on his face like he had shared a deep, dark secret that helped explain the very essence of anger and even life itself. Max stood there proudly as some quiet giggles began to break the silence. I could see by looking at Max that the little light bulb had gone off in his head telling him how his last statement sounded. Being the smooth, composed, professional speaker he was, Max decided to clarify his previous remark.

"Not *these* balls," Max grabbed himself as a visual aid to demonstrate what he was *not* talking about. "I don't paint *these* balls," Max said as he grabbed himself again.

Just then, the teacher piped in. "Circles, Max. You mean you paint *circles*!"

"Yes, circles. I paint circles when I'm angry," said Max. "See?" He held up his painting.

Max then returned to his seat with the satisfied look of someone who thought, "I nailed that." Meanwhile, the teacher had a look on her face that said, "Now I need to bump up the sex ed. component of the curriculum." Funny enough, the teacher invited me back for the remainder of the program.

I got the opportunity to work with Max for three more years. To my knowledge, Max never painted again. I hope it wasn't a permanent scar left from this episode. He did move on to playing with balls. Max was a very accomplished athlete during his sixth-, seventh-, and eighth-grade school years and seemed to use that as a healthy outlet for his emotions. After all, art isn't for everyone.

CHAPTER FIVE
Living a Privileged Life

"When you're accustomed to privilege, equality feels like oppression."

—Brian Sims

During the fall of 2007, while I was busy keeping up with the hectic school schedule, my family received some exciting news. My mother was buying a house! It was big news because, at sixty years old, my mother was purchasing her first home. I mentioned before that I have been lucky to be surrounded by strong women in my personal life. For years, these women have been modeling for me what powerful, independent women look like. More importantly, they have been doing the exact same thing for my daughter, adding yet another strong woman to my life.

I'm lucky to have a grandmother, two mothers, two sisters, and a wife who have each taught me about female perspective. It's probably a big reason why the thought of walking in women's shoes and entering my new career wasn't as threatening or intimidating to me as it could be for others. Strong women have always been in my life, and they are a big part of the inspiration for this recollection. The thought of any of them being hurt or mistreated motivates me to keep addressing the issue of violence against women and the factors that contribute to it.

My mother was preparing to move from her apartment—her home of over twenty years—to her first purchased house. Naturally, I was going to be there to help her. Arrangements were made, and I drove two hours to her apartment to help her prepare and move the following day. Little did I know, there was going to be extra stress associated with her move since she was leaving an apartment building. I also wasn't prepared for the stress being exacerbated because she was a single woman. The night before the move, I worked with my mom to pack, clean, and even remove carpet she had laid on the floor.

The following day, the movers she had hired would arrive and the official move would begin. Before that, there were some final details. As I was stripping carpet, there was a knock at the door, and my mom left me to work alone so she could answer it. I was busy and wasn't really focused on the conversation until I heard the voices get louder. I could sense the tension in the air and knew something was amiss. I stopped my work and listened.

"I'm sorry, Christine, but you can't monopolize the elevator. Your movers will have to use the stairs," the apartment superintendent said.

"And because of that, your bill for the move will go up considerably." I assumed this must be someone from the moving company.

"You have people move in and out of this building all the time. I've never seen people use the stairs," my mom replied. "I've been living here for over twenty years. All I'm asking for is a little respect as I leave."

"There is nothing I can do. The rules are the rules. You're moving during the week, and people need the elevator," the superintendent responded.

The conversation continued for another minute or so with neither side budging. I could hear my mother getting more and more upset as the bad news continued and felt she might need a helping hand.

I casually walked by the open door and calmly said, "Is everything okay, Mom?"

I will never forget the immediate change in tone. It was like the superintendent and the mover instantly gained some respect for my mother.

"Listen, Christine, I'm sure we can work something out. I'll tell you what, you can use the elevator as long as it isn't completely unavailable to others." The superintendent said this a little louder to ensure I heard him.

"We'll make sure we move quickly and maximize each load. Since we can use the elevator, the estimate we gave you for the move will be the same," the mover added.

Just like that, the problem was solved. I was astounded. How did the conversation turn so quickly? Why was the elevator such an issue and then suddenly not? The only thing I could point to was my presence. Simply because they knew I was there, they had treated my mother with more respect. It was disgusting and unbelievable to me, but upon further reflection, what was even more disturbing to me was … I *liked* it.

I felt proud my presence had turned the tide for my mother. Of course, I said all the right things to my mom. I told her how wrong it was (and I truly meant it). I listened as she said that, for a single woman, it was normal and she wasn't completely surprised. I supported her and was happy I could be there for her. I was also glad it had happened when I was there and that I had prevented this wrong from continuing. But what had I *really* done? I had walked by the door. I had spoken in my "manly" voice. I hadn't done anything other than be a male.

The problem was sexism. The men at the door may not have been consciously sexist, but it seemed to be the only logical explanation. But the other problem was, I *liked* playing the hero, and the only thing that made me the hero was my gender. This is also an example of sexism. I imagine I stood a little taller that night. I suspect I spoke more confidently. Shamefully, I know I felt like more of a man.

The fact that male privilege exists in our society is a problem. But the bigger problem is many men—often without knowing it—*like* the fact it exists. Good men. These are men who don't notice they like it because they've never had to think about it. That was me. I considered myself to be a good man. But if I didn't really understand the issue of violence against women and the systemic sexism that causes it, how could I truly be part of the solution?

This was a pivotal moment for me. It was the time other parts of feminism started to become clearer to me. It's the little things that quite often add up to become the larger issue. I think many men like feeling they can solve women's problems by metaphorically riding in on the horse to save the day. But if men feel women need rescuing (even subconsciously), and they like the feeling of doing the rescuing, how can we ever see women as equals? If women are often the punch lines to jokes, how can we truly treat them with complete and utter respect? This is a large part of the systemic sexism that exists in our culture.

It's that sexism that was culminating in the stories I heard so often from the women I encountered in the community. When I started my new job in the VAW field, my view on violence against women was simplistic. Now, I understand it's not simply an evil or bad man hurting or abusing his wife, girlfriend, or daughter out of anger. It is a cycle of power and control passed on from generation to generation. The issue is very complex and deep-rooted. This is something I was learning and would continue to learn. It was also something I felt I needed to share with other men. I was about to get that chance as I entered another chapter of my education. I was about to start working with boys and men.

CHAPTER SIX
It's a Dad's Life

"My father didn't teach me how to live; he lived and let me watch him do it."

—Clarence Budington Kelland

A large factor in my organization's decision to break new ground and hire a male (me) into the VAW field was their desire to engage boys and men in conversations about how to build healthy relationships and end violence. It was thought by the powers that be that a male would have more success connecting with a male audience than a female. This wasn't something I gave much thought to as I entered my new role. But after more than a decade on the job, I have come to the realization they were right. It's something I experience all the time. My female co-worker has been called a "power-tripping feminist" for saying the exact same things I say in class. Me? Well, I'm called a leader, a role model, and a confident speaker when I read from the exact same lesson plan as my co-worker.

I truly believe some of the things I say sound more like the rant of the stereotypical feminist than anything my female co-workers ever say. But I get away with it because of my gender. This is yet another example of the male privilege I am afforded. But, since the privilege exists, I have decided I will use it to try to forward the agenda of gender equality. That might sound bizarre, but if male privilege can be used to oppress, then we should use that same privilege for whatever positive things we can. Maybe we can use that privilege to end it altogether.

With the goal of engaging a male audience in mind, I was given the additional responsibility of creating and facilitating boys groups and a program specifically for dads. The dads group gave me the most reason for pause. Talking to students was one thing, but I was being asked to go into a room with adult men and talk about being the best father possible.

On the surface, it sounded logical. I was a dad, and I took that role more seriously than any other job I'd ever had. Talking about it with other dads made perfect sense to me, but when I thought of *doing* it, I got very nervous and concerned about how I would accomplish it. I mean, what could I do? Talk about feelings? Draw pictures? Listen to the song "Cat's in the Cradle"? No, I couldn't do that—or could I?

Believe it or not, that's exactly what I did. I gave the dads surveys evaluating their own fathers so they could reflect on how their male role models had shaped their parenting strategies. I also had the men trace their hands and write their struggles or worries about being a father on each finger. And yes, we did all this while I played "Cat's in the Cradle" in the background.

When I look back on these initial attempts at talking to a group of men about parenting, I cringe, but I also laugh. How could I have had the guts to try some of those things? It was because I *did* have the guts (out of pure desperation) that some of them worked. No, we didn't start listing to Harry Chapin songs each week. In fact, after a couple of wobbly attempts, the song was mercifully discarded.

Amazingly enough, the groups became some of my favorite things. They also became very popular among some of the local dads. I started getting regulars each time the group was offered. When I expanded the group to include children and dinner, things really took off. The dads really seemed to enjoy the idea of bringing their children to a group, pumping them full of pizza and pop, and then handing them off to moms afterward. I can probably guess how the moms felt about it. But in all seriousness, as the group developed and progressed, the discussions became increasingly authentic and meaningful. It was becoming more and more clear that all these men needed was a place to talk.

"Well, it was a rough week for me, guys," a participant named Chuck shared with the group. "It was doughnut week at school."

This was before nutritional guidelines became the norm in schools.

Chuck continued venting, "My daughter reminded me on Tuesday to make sure to give her a dollar to buy a doughnut, and of course, I forgot. I mean, it was a busy week and a busy morning. So she gets home after school and freaks out! Like missing out on a doughnut is the worst thing that could ever happen. I offered to take her for a bloody doughnut, but all she did was complain all night. She's still pissed at me."

The group often became a place to vent and discuss our successes and failures as fathers. It was amazing to see the initial awkwardness of a group turn into genuine support and camaraderie. The group usually started out stiff with looks that said, "I can't believe I'm actually here." The members would even share their displeasure with comments like, "The only reason I'm here is because my wife told me to come." I think that was the most common reason many men came at first. But once a group got going, it was almost always successful, and it genuinely helped the dads think about what they were doing well and what they could do better. In my opinion, the fact these men took the time to attend a group for fathers already put them pretty high on the list of good parents.

"So it was doughnut week again, and I really thought about what we talked about last week. You know, how it's the little things that often make the biggest difference for our kids," Chuck shared with the group.

"You remembered to give your daughter the dollar this time?" I offered hopefully.

"Nope. Completely forgot again," Chuck answered. "But do you know what I did instead? I remembered after she left, so I climbed on my motorcycle and went and bought her favorite doughnut. I showed up at the school during first recess. She saw me sitting on my bike, and I held up the bag and gave it a wave. Man, she ran to me and gave me the biggest hug. It was the first time she'd hugged me in public in years!"

The small things often make the biggest difference.

Little did I know, this group was also going to give me the opportunity to dispel some misconceptions about the work done within a VAW agency. It was during the third time running the group I encountered a very angry dad named Troy.

Troy was mad about a lot of different things, but mostly about his ex-wife. He was in the middle of an ugly custody battle with her and thought attending the group would look good to the courts. Troy was the classic reluctant participant. During the first session, he sat with his arms crossed, shoulders scrunched, and sported a large and unmistakable scowl. When asked why he was attending the group, Troy semi-grunted. "Gotta do the song and dance so I can see my kids."

Troy was largely unresponsive during the first session, and truth be told, I didn't think I'd see him again. To my surprise, he returned the next week, albeit with the same gruff demeanor. To his credit, he came to the group again and again. In fact, he became a regular attendee every time the group was offered. It seemed Troy had initially come for the optics but was now coming because he wanted to.

A common topic for Troy was about arguments and conflict with his ex-wife. When this topic arose, Troy was often in the middle of the conversation and was genuinely interested in the different perspectives offered by the other fathers. Based on his reactions, it was becoming obvious he had moved past worrying about what his lawyer or the judge would think of him attending the group and was now focusing more on his children. Troy became so invested, he often asked for handouts and more information when the group sessions ended. I left the last session feeling pretty good about the group and what Troy had taken from it. I hoped he would be able to use what we'd talked about to make things healthier for himself, his ex-wife, and most of all, his children. But I couldn't be sure. That is, until later that week when Troy called.

"I'm really struggling. I don't want to yell or scream. I want to work with my ex-wife better, but I just don't know how. I don't want my kids to suffer. Can we meet up and talk?"

I suggested he come to my office. I could tell from his response he was uncertain about coming to where I worked. But Troy did come to my office, and it quickly became apparent he felt like he had entered a whole new world.

"You know, I never thought I would ever be in this building. I didn't even think I'd be allowed in here."

There are several dangerous misconceptions about VAW work. One misconception is that the people who work there hate men. Another is that the organization's goal is to break up families. From my experience, these things simply aren't true. Speaking as the only man who works in my VAW agency, they certainly don't hate men, and the last thing that they want to do is break up families. They simply want *healthy* families. I've known that for a long time, and it was nice to see another man could (maybe) see that as well.

Troy and I talked that day and on a few other occasions in the weeks and months that followed. The meetings always took place at my office, and I could see he was becoming more comfortable entering the building. During his last visit to my office, he asked a question that had obviously been on his mind for quite a while.

"I've been wondering why the doors are locked here. Why do you have to be buzzed in?"

I explained the dangers some of the residents faced.

"The locked doors and security are in place to make sure the women who live here are safe," I said.

Troy took a few seconds and seemed to be mulling something over in his mind. "I noticed some small monuments in the gardens with names on them. What are they all about?"

"Those are some women and children who have died at their partners' and fathers' hands because of violence," I responded.

I could see everything he thought about where I worked and who I worked for was changing. He was starting to see the benefit of—and the need for—an organization like the one with which I was involved. It wasn't only Troy's attitude toward my employer that was changing. He was also working really hard to make sure he co-parented with his ex-wife to the best of his abilities. All it took was for people to listen to him, a safe place to do it, and some different perspectives.

As I mentioned before, it's difficult to understand the issues when you don't know they exist. The dads group taught me about motivating factors. To truly engage men in trying to stop violence against women, we need to help them understand what is at stake. That can be a sister, mother, female friend, and even a daughter. Every woman is important to someone, so every woman should be important to us all.

Troy went on to improve his parenting relationship with his ex-wife, and hopefully, passed some of his new-found perspective on to his son and daughter. I'll never forget the look on his face the day he started to do what I had been doing for a couple of years: walk in a woman's shoes. Even if it was for just a moment.

CHAPTER SEVEN
You want me to do what?

"The more you know, the more you realize how much you don't know."

—David T. Freeman

With the success of the dads group and a popular school-based program, I found myself becoming busier and busier. As a result, another educator was hired and added to our team. It just so happened it was a male. This was a large bonus for me because I now had a co-facilitator for some of the gender-specific groups. He was also a great guy who shared many of my values and opinions. On top of that, Neil was one of the funniest people I had ever met. He provided a lot of much-needed comedic relief during some stressful situations. Neil would jump out of large cardboard boxes to startle you, move your entire desk to another room, and we even wore matching Santa suits to our holiday party one year.

One stressful situation I could use some support with (and some humor) was about to arise due to the popularity of the dads groups. My manager called me into her office on a Monday morning to discuss a new and exciting opportunity. The agency had been contacted by the local Parent and Child Center about our dads program. This seemed of little significance to me since we had done the programs there many times. As much as I enjoyed the dads groups, I was unclear about what was new or exciting about this announcement.

They wanted a group facilitator to talk to their moms. What was *supposed* to be exciting was they wanted a male perspective. Of course, there was one final wrinkle added to the equation: the moms in the group were all dealing with some form of postpartum depression. Remember when I mentioned the anxiety and uncertainty that surrounded my entering an all-female, ninth-grade health class? Well, multiply that by 1000 and you have some sense of where I was in that moment. Luckily, I now had a male counterpart who could go with me.

"Hey, Neil, I need you to come with me to a postpartum depression group next week," I told him later that day.

"I didn't know men got postpartum depression."

"It's not for men. We are going to a moms group. They want a dad's perspective on parenting."

Neil took a second to process this exciting news.

"You *do* know I'm not a father yet, right?" Neil answered.

"Yes, but I'm sure as hell not doing this alone. Congratulations. You're coming with me!"

So off we went. A newly-married man without children and a man with one child were going to impart our parenting wisdom to a group of new mothers. To be honest, it sounded like a recipe for disaster.

"Don't worry, Neil. It'll be fun," I said without too much conviction.

"This does not feel fun," Neil muttered.

If I were being honest, I had to agree with him. A feeling of impending doom sat firmly upon my shoulders. I had managed to stumble my way through my initial attempts at a dads group, but that was in part because *I* was a dad. How could we possibly manage our way through this?

What was our plan? Well, we decided to start with an activity that involved labeled cups. Each cup represented something parents had to balance—things like children, paying bills, their partner, and household chores. We were going to get the moms to stack the cups with what was most important to them on the top of the pile. Then we were going to get them to do it again, but this time, they would have only fifteen seconds to do it. The whole point was to demonstrate how our priorities sometimes changed simply because of the hectic schedule of life. Our hope was to inspire some sort of conversation and uncover some of the things they wanted to discuss. Our "big plan" was cup stacking for adults. Now you understand why we were scared.

With the butterflies seemingly making a permanent home in our stomachs, we got set up and waited for the moms to arrive.

"Do you ever think about what we do?" Neil continued without waiting for a response. "I can't imagine any other men in the world doing some of the things we do all the time. Think about it. We're about to sit with a group of moms and give them a man's perspective on parenting. When I tell my brother or dad about my day, they look at me like I'm crazy."

"It is pretty unique, I'll give you that," I answered.

I had never really stopped to think about how unique my job was. When I stopped to think about it, I didn't imagine there were many men who worked in an almost exclusively female environment with the focus on addressing the issue of violence against women. When you combine that with the different audiences and groups we talked to, it probably did make it a very rare job opportunity.

The time for those deep, introspective thoughts would have to come later because just then, the door opened and the moms entered. It may seem silly, but as they marched in (and it did seem like they marched), I silently hummed the Darth Vader theme from *Star Wars* in my head. Not to be overly dramatic, but that feeling of impending doom I spoke of earlier did seem to increase exponentially the moment the door opened. That feeling didn't subside as the women stopped to look at us because one woman spoke up before Neil or I opened our mouths.

"So we hear you two are the parenting experts."

I've had many reluctant participants before: angry-looking dads, disinterested-looking eighth-grade students, and even teenagers sleeping in the classroom. I found this group more than a little unnerving. I looked around the room and saw eight women with their arms crossed as they stared directly at the two of us. I glanced over at Neil and almost laughed at the sheer terror on his face. He had run his hands through his hair so it looked all mussed, and he stared straight ahead. We all sat there for what felt like an eternity just looking at each other.

Neil was the one who finally broke the silence. When he spoke, he sounded as panicked as he looked. "I'm sorry. I'm not actually a parent."

That didn't seem to ease the tension. The seconds ticked away, and I thought I'd better come up with a better introduction than "I'm not a parent." I worked up some courage and was about to begin when one of the women interjected.

"We're just messing with you. We're glad you're here."

The women laughed, and Neil and I nervously joined them as we both breathed a sigh of relief and began to unclench every part of our bodies. The group turned into one of most enjoyable experiences I've ever had. We did our little cup activity, and the moms absolutely loved it. There was very little effort required to get them talking—in fact, there was no effort needed at all. The entire time, a part of me was thinking about how easy it seemed. The women talked freely, without any kind of hesitation. It was so different from the dads group, which is always so initially awkward and uncomfortable for everyone. It's true this group was also awkward in the beginning, but that was just a joke being played on two nervous, unsuspecting guys.

As we continued the group, I began to feel sorry for the dads and for many men in general. I thought to myself that it must be so freeing to share your thoughts and emotions. I thought, "Wouldn't it be nice (and healthier) if men felt that same comfort when talking to other men?"

I began to wonder when boys and men start to become less social and when barriers to sharing their feelings are formed. The experience with the moms group was eye-opening. If I'm being honest, I think the group did more for Neil and me than we did for the moms. I'm not sure how much help we were to them. When one mom asked how she could get her husband to come to the table when dinner was served, I mentioned I bang on a pot in my house when I've finished cooking dinner (they loved that). Neil's response to how to get men more involved in housework was even better.

"I recently found a dishwasher on the side of the road, and it looked like it was in good shape. I rolled it home, and now I don't have to do the dishes," he said.

Some of the women laughed so hard, I swear they almost wet themselves. To sum it all up, we taught the women how to stack cups, look for used dishwashers, and bang on pots. You just can't make this stuff up! But the group must have been of some use to the moms because we were asked to come back to work with another group a few months later. In fact, it started to become a regular thing. We were asked by two other centers to share our program (our cup-stacking road show was now called a "program"). In total, we did twelve different moms groups in two years. Neil became a dad during this time and seemed much more confident in his parenting tips.

Eventually, due to several factors that included our busy school schedule and Neil moving on to a new job opportunity, the moms group came to an end. The lessons I learned during that time were not forgotten though. I will always cherish those easy and open conversations. I will always want men and boys to have that same sense of freedom and openness when it comes to sharing their emotions and feelings.

POSTSCRIPT:

Neil worked with me for over five years. He was an incredible sounding board, confidant, co-worker, and friend during his time as my colleague. There is no one I'd rather address a group of reluctant dads with. He is the only one who can ever truly understand the ups and downs of a couple of guys running a postpartum depression parenting group with some new moms.

CHAPTER EIGHT
The Big Bleed-Through

"The most wasted of all days is one without laughter."

—E.E. Cummings

I said it before, and I'll say it again, the organization I work for likes meetings. I'm not talking about the quick thirty-minute meeting. I'm talking about the two-and-a-half hour, get-comfortable-and-bring-a-snack type of meeting. I mention snacks because they have always been as important to the meeting as the people themselves. In fact, the most critical role assigned for each meeting was the person responsible for bringing the elaborate snack. When I first sat through one of these meetings, a few things happened. My rear end went numb, my back stiffened, and my mind wandered. Coming from the business world, we had a singular purpose for our meetings. Address the issues, come up with a solution, and move on. Rarely did a meeting ever stretch beyond an hour in my previous life. So when I entered the second hour of my first meeting in my new job, I began ask myself some questions.

"How long can this last?"

"Don't we all have things to do?"

"Is anyone else really sore?"

"They can't really have more snacks to share, can they?"

But what I quickly realized was, in this line of work where exposure to grief, pain, and trauma is the norm, these types of meetings are not only important but necessary. It's how people who work with the saddest and most disturbing situations in the world stay so amazingly optimistic. They care for themselves and each other. Somehow, in a place that sees abuse, sexual assault, and violence, there is a feeling of hope. Never a day goes by without hearing someone laugh hysterically. You rarely walk by someone without receiving a warm smile and a greeting, and when people ask how you're doing, they actually stop and *want* to know the answer.

It took me a while to get used to this and understand how it was possible. But after a while, I was able to connect some dots and realize the meetings and social connections were how the women who worked here not only survived but thrived. The two-and-a-half hours each week weren't as much about business and case management as they were about self-care and supporting each other. By connecting and leaning on one another, they gained strength from the relationships they were nurturing. In a place that counseled and taught people about healthy relationships, they were living the actual example, and I was witnessing the benefits.

I grew to look forward to our weekly meetings. But what I didn't know was they were merely an appetizer for something bigger and more intense. That would be the "All-Staff" meeting. This was held twice a year on the first Wednesday in November and June. It would bring together all the different departments off-site to connect and meet for the entire day. It was an opportunity for training, agency business and, of course, team building, support and—wait for it—food! I had thought the weekly meetings were an eye-opener, but the All-Staff meetings were an even bigger surprise. We did a lot of work at the All-Staff meetings and participated in some amazing training opportunities. We also:

- Made chocolate
- Did laugh yoga

- Threw eggs off buildings
- Wore garbage bags while we tried to slurp up whipped cream

Those were only the morning sessions. The All-Staff day was an experience like no other. It was the only time I was able see everyone I worked with. It was also the only time I was reminded I was the only male in the organization. If I didn't notice during the meeting sessions, it became quite apparent during break time when my co-workers were lined up to use the washroom and I had a private one. It was also often mentioned when we had a guest speaker. Most speakers seemed to feel the need to give me my own welcome: "Good morning, ladies … and to you too over there!" Beyond those times, however, my exclusivity as the sole male employee at these meetings was rarely an issue. I say rarely because, once in a while, it did become a big part of the day.

We were often split into small work groups during the All-Staff meeting. This was done at the start of the day to get us warmed up for the day's events and information. During one particular warm-up, we had the goal of learning more about our co-workers. The activity was quite simple; we had to make a list of things everyone in your group had done. Someone was to say something, and if every person in the group could say they had done that thing, it was recorded. Immediately, people starting yelling ideas so the group could get as many things recorded as possible. There were often prizes for these games, and they were usually food-based, so the stakes were high.

"Have we all slept on the ground?"

"Yes," we all responded. Then we had a few more matches in succession.

"We've all traveled outside of Canada."

"Yes!"

"Each of us has a child."

"We all do."

"We all have owned a pet."

"I have three."

"Everyone here has been to the hospital."

"Naturally, we all have."

"Of course, we've all had a bleed-through."

Wait, what? I didn't put my hand up for that. But the group kept going, rapid-fire style, naming things quickly, and I had to move past that one to keep up. Before I knew what was happening, the time for the activity was up and our list was made. The next thing I knew, our group was asked to read our list aloud. The rule of the game was any other group could challenge your list by asking any member of the group a question to make sure everyone had, in fact, done or experienced it. You can probably guess what happened next.

Our list was reviewed without challenge or incident until … the bleed-through.

"We have also all experienced a bleed-through. But that was easy because everyone in the room has gone through that," our group presenter told the rest of the staff.

"Well, not everybody," corrected one co-worker.

Giggles followed and echoed around the room. It was just then my group seemed to notice my presence for the first time.

"Oh my God. I'm so sorry, Travis." My group presenter blushed.

"Honestly, I didn't know what you were talking about. I assumed I hadn't experienced it, but I didn't have time to tell everyone," I answered.

When I reflect on the incident, I think a few things happened to our team during that activity.

The focus on the food prize and competitive juices got the best of the group. Food did always seem to be a big motivator for the people I worked with.

I wasn't as assertive as I needed to be.

Communication wasn't really clear.

For just a few minutes, the fact I was male was forgotten.

I've noticed that a few times over the years in my agency. Sometimes, the women I work with get so used to working exclusively with female co-workers, they forget I'm different. I love it when that happens. For a little while, I'm not the only man working in the building. For a moment, we are all just people working together. I think equality truly happens when we don't see differences; we simply see people. I would love to see our society get to that point. That's easy for a white male to say because differences don't negatively impact my life for the most part. It would be a nice place to get to. But, as the amazing women I work with have shown me, we have a long way to go before we get there. Until then, I will remember the day I learned about the "bleed-through."

POSTSCRIPT:

I thought of titling the book "The Big Bleed-Through" because the term was so foreign to me, and it obviously represented a different experience from my own. Thankfully, I have people in my life who are much wiser than I am. My daughter convinced me to go another route.

"Oh gross, Dad. Sometimes you're such a guy. You can call it that, but I'm not buying a copy."

CHAPTER NINE

Man Up!

"The three most destructive words that every man receives when he's a boy is when he's told to 'be a man.'"

—Joe Ehrmann

"I'd like all of the boys who have cried before to raise their hands."

A nervous silence fell over the room. Boys began to look at each other almost silently daring someone to raise their hand. Finally, after a few nervous seconds, a boy casually raised his hand and said very nonchalantly, "I cried when I was a baby."

Laughter followed as the rest of the boys raised their hands with shouts of, "Me too," and "Yeah, I did when I was a baby."

As things began to settle down, I asked another question. "Can the boys please raise their hand if they have cried within the last month?"

Now things were getting uncomfortable. The boys were no longer looking at each other. They simply stared at the ground, completely silent. That is, until one young man raised his hand.

"Well, I cried when my parents split up," he said, his voice uncertain.

No one said anything for a moment. The comment simply hung in the air, and no one seemed to know how to react. The tension grew as tears fill the boy's eyes and slowly start to fall down his cheeks. Then a sound emanated from the far side of the room. At first, people didn't know what it was. But as the other boys in the room heard the sound, it spread. The sound was laughter.

That scene played itself out in front of me during my first year working in classrooms. I watched a very courageous young man share his feelings only to be mocked and put down for it. It took place in a typical fifth-grade class, and it happened during a lesson I had run many times before. We were discussing gender stereotypes and how they can contribute to low self-esteem and even bullying and violence. The questions I asked of the boys that day were questions I had asked many times before and hundreds of times since. The initial reactions I received in this class were almost identical to what I have seen from other boys in many different classrooms. It's like they all read from the same script, and in a sense, I suppose they do.

The first question is almost always received with a little shock, awkward silence, giggles, and then the predictable "when I was a baby" response. The second question is often met with complete silence, little or no eye contact, and a very uncomfortable feeling.

This is usually when the discussion takes place that helps us navigate the damaging world of male stereotypes. We explore the stereotypical, media-driven image of modern-day masculinity. It is an image often built on toughness, aggression, and a complete lack of emotion (unless that emotion is anger). The experience of seeing firsthand how uncomfortable their male classmates are with their emotions is usually a very powerful lesson.

So what was different that day? Well ... what was different was a young man named Seth. Seth had the guts to tell the truth and share how he felt. This caught everyone in the room—including me—off guard. It wasn't expected, it wasn't typical, and it wasn't ... normal. As I have seen many times since, when the young boys in that room became uncomfortable or unsure of how to react, they reverted to the male default setting as created by our culture. They made it into a joke. When a young boy expressed his feelings of sadness and grief, the response he received was ridicule. It's no wonder boys, and eventually men, become reluctant to share their feelings in our society. They feel exposed and at risk. As I saw in that classroom, the risk is very real.

So there I was, in a room full of students who were laughing at a boy who silently cried. The students seemed to be so insensitive and programmed by stereotypes that they simply didn't appear to care about Seth. At least, that's what I thought.

It's very easy to get caught up with the negativity of a situation. Sometimes, due to that negativity, we can't see the positive things occurring right in front of our eyes. I was so focused on the laughter, I neglected to see a large portion of the class *not* laughing. In that moment, I didn't see the look of concern and disgust on many of the students' faces. They were as horrified and upset by the response as I was. I will never forget what happened next.

The sound of a chair being pushed back from a desk interrupted the laughter and giggles. A very well-liked girl named Sara stood and walked across the classroom to where Seth was standing. Without hesitation, Sara put her arm around Seth and gave him a half hug.

Then she said very loudly while staring at the other students, "Don't worry, Seth. Girls like guys who show their feelings."

The laughter stopped immediately, and an uneasy silence fell over the room. Since many of the boys had a crush on Sara, it now looked liked many of them wanted to cry.

"Man Up." "Be a Man." We hear these phrases all the time. But what do they really mean? Well, it depends on who you ask. Popular culture would have you believe it means the heroic, muscle-clad leading man—the man who shows no emotions and leads by sheer will and physical force. This definition of masculinity certainly sells movie tickets and builds television ratings, but it also can lead to a society full of boys and men who are taught to deny their emotions. Unfortunately, denying them doesn't mean they don't exist. They still manifest themselves in some form, and that form is often aggression and violence.

Many people don't see how much male stereotypes hurt our society. They certainly hurt women, as evidenced by the fact our shelter is full of women leaving abusive partners every day (most often male partners). But they also hurt men. There are men and boys who feel isolated, alone, and ashamed if they don't measure up to the male stereotype of toughness and aggression.

Contrary to popular belief, boys are not born violent. Think about a four-year-old boy. When he's hurt, he cries. He's not afraid to tell his dad he loves him. Now think about that same boy when he's fourteen. When he's hurt, he holds it in. It becomes awkward to tell his dad he loves him.

No, boys aren't born violent; we teach them to be violent. Those lessons start early and continue to get refined and more specific as boys get older. They learn those lessons from the media, sometimes at home, and often from their peers. These messages can cause men to hurt women and hurt themselves. As much as the work I do with boys and girls in classrooms is important, a more important thing that must be done is to work specifically with boys. We will never truly affect change until we allow our sons to be who they authentically are, until we give them the freedom to be themselves and feel what they feel. We need them to be like Seth, and we need to make sure they aren't punished for it.

Seth and Sara have never left my heart. One of them was a boy who had the guts to be himself. The other was a girl who knew what she stood for and, more importantly, what she wouldn't stand for. In my opinion, we need more boys and girls like Seth and Sara in this world, and I truly believe education is the only way to make that happen. That's why I have never doubted my decision to enter the world of feminism and VAW work. It has helped me learn things about the world that I didn't know before. It's also given me the platform to share what I have learned with countless boys and girls. Sometimes, sharing that knowledge would be as difficult as it was for Seth to stand there in front of a group of guys and cry. That's because I was about to enter the world of working exclusively with boys.

CHAPTER TEN
Hanging with the Boys

"Would the boy you were be proud of the man you became?"

—Laurence J. Peter

WARNING:

Some readers may find this chapter disturbing. There may be terms or language used that may be confusing or upsetting. Reader discretion is advised. That may seem slightly alarming and a tad on the extreme side of things, but I've learned you can never be too prepared when you are working with a group of boys.

'The boys group—the final frontier.'

That's a revised quote from one of my favorite shows. Yes, I love *Star Trek*, and yes, I'm a Trekkie. But take it from me, that quote is appropriate. Boys groups *are* the final frontier. In my line of work, they are the true test. It's like what they say about New York. "If you can make it there, you can make it anywhere." The same is true about running a boys group.

When I started in my new career, I had a full head of hair. Over ten years of boys groups have accounted for the significant loss of my once-proud hair empire. Every time I think I've seen it all in a boys group, I am corrected by a new group of guys. Fist fights, crying, a guy trapped in the girls' bathroom, homework hidden in the ceiling, the braiding of armpit hair, and most of all, fun and transformations. But it's a long journey to get to the true objectives of a boys group. I don't want to generalize because all people are different, and thus, all groups are different. What is amazing is how many groups start out the same way.

It usually starts with a group of panic-stricken boys entering a room like they are making the last walk of their lives. Nervously looking at the ground, they sit in a circle formation I've created. I always start by asking the boys why they are here or what they think the group is about. The answers vary but usually all stay true to a common theme.

"It's a group for kids who are in trouble."

"We need extra help."

"This is where the bad students get sent."

Of course, none of these things are true. When I run a boys group in a school, I simply ask the organizer to put together a group of guys who could benefit from some socialization and leadership skills. Yet, over and over, if boys are asked to be in a group, they automatically assume it's because they are bad, messed up, or broken.

It sits in sharp contrast to the girls groups my female counterpart runs. In those groups, the girls almost always see it as an opportunity. They see the value in participating in a group. I've learned boys don't see it the same way. They don't see the opportunity; they see a potential threat.

The boys often see the risks associated with the group. What they seem to fear most is being seen as weak or vulnerable or having to talk about their feelings, so I do my best to try to put the group at ease. I talk about the group being whatever they want it to be. It can be deep and meaningful. It can be personal, educational, or simply a fun place to hang out. You can probably guess what most guys choose it to be.

This signifies the second stage of a boys group. I call it the "lifting the leg" stage. This stage is similar to when a male dog lifts his leg as high as he can to pee so the other dogs can see his dominance. Thankfully, there haven't been any documented cases of urinating in the group, but there is a lot of posturing. What I see most is when a boy feels uncomfortable, he turns to either aggression or humor. Thankfully, most times in the group, it's humor.

"Name one thing you like about yourself," I said during a self-esteem session.

There have been serious and authentic answers, but most often the answers follow the "lift the leg" theory.

"I like that I can eat a lot of tacos."

"What I like most is my KDR and ability to kill n00bs." Translation: I like my kill-to-death ratio and ability to kill new players in *Call of Duty*.

"I like my shlong." Translation: Not just used to describe the penis but one with considerable length.

Welcome to the boys groups.

It usually surprises the boys most when I simply go with what they are saying. For example, if I'm recording the things they like about themselves, those things get written down (yes, all of those things). I have come to learn the boys are looking for a reaction of shock, anger, or for some sort of punishment or penalty to be handed out. If we truly want to engage boys, however, we need to meet them where they are. If I don't react in a negative way, the boys become a little unsure of things. It is quickly made apparent the regular rules of a boy's world don't apply here.

Boys usually put on a show for each other because they get positive attention from their peers. Most understand negative attention from an adult is often a side effect of this, but they are willing to take that in exchange for acceptance from their peers. In fact, the negative adult attention sometimes elevates them more in the eyes of their male friends. That dynamic needs to be reset if the group has any hope of being successful.

They receive the stereotypical messages early, so it takes a while for any significant change to be seen. Sometimes, it takes weeks of juvenile games, outrageous comments, and making things into jokes before we begin to peel back that initial layer of insecurity. It's during these times I imagine what this group would look like to an objective observer. I think I would probably look like an overworked circus ringmaster trying to maintain some semblance of order in a circus tent of chaos.

Most people, if they peeked into a boys group during the first few weeks, would wonder what possible good could come from it. Sometimes, I wonder the same thing. This is especially true when I look through the window to the adjoining classroom and see my female co-worker running the girls group. The girls all look so serious sitting in a circle and sharing. I often feel a pang of jealousy and wonder what I'm doing wrong.

It's usually around this time my boys are flipping water bottles or trying to figure out who farted. However, it's also during this time small nuggets of truth begin to seep into the group. These are the moments when the boys show you who they truly are. It could be something simple like a couple of them staying after group to help clean up. It might be when one of them answers a question seriously, or someone shares something that happened to him in the past week, or maybe a group member offers encouragement to one of the other guys.

This is when attention is given and a big deal is made out of what they are doing. *This* is when the quality of authenticity becomes entrenched. The entire goal of the group is for boys to feel comfortable being their authentic selves. If this can be accomplished, then we begin to address the larger goal of building healthy relationships and preventing violence. It's when we can begin to make significant changes for individuals and communities at large.

One activity that seems to really allow boys to discover who they are is something called a "Values Auction." This activity gives them the opportunity to think about what they want their lives to be like. An auction sheet is given to each boy along with $1000 in Monopoly money. The auction list has things on it the boys may want in their lives. There are superficial things like a cool car, a big house, or popularity. Then there are deeper things someone may want like health, respect, or a healthy relationship with their partner. The boys are given some time to consider what things they want most and plan how much of their money they are willing to spend on each item. The boys could choose to buy things on the sheet or save their money for something called "A Secret Prize." The Secret Prize always drove the guys crazy. They would almost always ask, "What is a Secret Prize?"

"It's called a Secret Prize because I can't tell you what it is," I would respond cryptically.

The whole idea was to make the boys choose between what they truly wanted or risk it for the great unknown. In truth, the Secret Prizes varied between good and bad things to reinforce this lesson if a boy decided to save his money for that. In summation, the guys would need to plan and prioritize carefully because they could only buy things until they ran out of money. As mentioned, this activity really seemed to resonate with them. I remember one time when a boy really discovered his authentic self during the auction.

Tyler was the group clown and took his role of being completely unserious *very* seriously. Tyler did things like hide his weekly homework in the ceiling tiles, make farting noises during discussions, and somehow got wedged between the wall and a toilet in the stall of the girls' bathroom. Week after week, Tyler would try to be more and more outrageous, and I could see him looking for my reaction. I could almost see him asking himself, "What do I have to do to get kicked out?" To be honest, it did cross my mind. But how could I kick a boy out of a group for doing the very things he was in the group to work on? Plus, Tyler had the option of quitting anytime he wanted to, so the fact he was still coming each week had to mean something.

With that said, Tyler was working on my last bit of patience as the group passed the halfway mark. I started to wonder if he might be one of the guys the group just didn't work for. Then we did the Values Auction. I handed out the supplies and quickly reviewed the things the boys were going to bid on. Each of the boys was to review their sheets and mark down a few things they were going to try to purchase. It was then that I noticed things had gotten really quiet. In fact, it had gotten eerily quiet. I wasn't sure what was missing at first, and then I realized Tyler's voice was missing. He wasn't talking or making any noises. Instead, he was studying his paper with the intensity of an air traffic controller studying a radar screen. It seemed this was an activity Tyler might take seriously, so off we went.

I tried to do my best impression of an auctioneer while the boys went wild with their money. They made it rain when they bought something, tried to jack up the price on something by bidding when they didn't really want it, and overall just had fun. That is, everyone except for Tyler. For the first time, he wasn't in the middle of everything.

He simply sat back and watched. He didn't bid, he didn't joke, and he didn't say a word. I was starting to wonder what was going on.

"Tyler, you haven't bid on anything yet," I commented.

"Nope," was his one-word response.

"Are you saving your money for a secret prize?" I asked.

"Nope," was once again his curt reply.

It was obvious something was on his mind, but with the organized chaos of the auction, it would have to wait until we were finished. We were down to the last three items on the auction list. The next item up for bid was "to have a healthy relationship with my partner." This is one item that sometimes gets a lot of bids, with some boys dreaming of marrying Jennifer Lawrence or Megan Fox. So the bidding began with a flourish.

"Do I have $100 for a healthy relationship with their partner?" I began in my fast-talking voice.

"$100 for Megan Fox!" yelled one boy.

"I'll pay $200," said another.

We got up to $500 pretty quickly, and it looked like the bidding might stop there. I started the countdown, "$500 going once, going twice ..."

"I'll pay $1000," said Tyler.

Everything suddenly got very quiet. Tyler was acting very seriously, which seemed to unnerve the group. He then stood and placed all his money on the table.

"Tyler, you can join the bidding and see if you can get it for less money. That way you'll still have some left over," I explained.

"No, thanks. That's all I really want."

I think this was the time someone would say, "Mic drop."

There was stunned silence in the room. As you can probably imagine, complete silence is a very rare occurrence in a boys group. The boys in the room didn't seem to know how to react. One of the most outrageous guys had just acted very seriously and had made a very significant statement. So what do boys do when they get uncomfortable? They turn to humor or ridicule.

"Oh, Tyler's going to get himself a honey!" someone yelled.

The next thing I knew, laughter and giggles rang out as the rest of the boys drew their own conclusions about what Tyler was saying with his purchase. To his credit, Tyler never flinched. He didn't react;

he just sat back in his chair looking very serious and very sure of himself. The lack of reaction from Tyler had the desired effect and quickly got everyone's attention.

"Why is that the only thing that you want, Tyler?" I asked.

"My mom has been with a bunch of jerks. They all treat her like crap. I would never treat my girlfriend like that. I want my life to be different," Tyler answered.

In more than ten years of doing boys groups, this is a moment I have never forgotten. Whenever I'm at my wit's end and have trouble seeing what good can possibly be happening in a group, I think of Tyler. I could have laid down the law with him. I could have removed him from the group. But if I had, he never would have experienced that moment. Just as important, the rest of the boys wouldn't have seen it either. What happened after Tyler's auction moment was a real discussion.

The other guys suddenly felt safe to share what they wanted from their lives. They talked about what they had experienced in their families and what they wanted their families to be like when they got older. This all happened because a young man decided to be himself. For a moment, he forgot about putting on a show for other people and thought about who he was and who he wanted to be.

I have learned boys and girls aren't that different from each other. It's true they often act very differently—just look at a boys group and a girls group on the same day. But how they act is more of an impact created by the world around them rather than a true reflection of the differences between boys and girls. Research shows when boys and girls are given the same psychological tests, their answers overlap by 90%. Sadly, it's the remaining 10% that is highlighted by our culture and mainstream media. It forces boys and girls into very narrowly-defined gender identities equipped with severe social penalties if they stray beyond the culturally-defined norm.

Tyler had the courage to challenge this norm. Instead of making a joke out of the activity, he chose to be authentic. Even when given the escape option by his group mates, he stuck with his beliefs. He didn't laugh along and say, "Yeah, I just want a hot wife!" He told the truth and was simply himself. This incident flies in the face of the old saying "boys will be boys." As Tyler demonstrated, the more accurate phrase is "boys will be … themselves." If we just let them.

My thoughts have changed from my first few years on the job. I had initially thought feminism was working to help women. But my experiences have taught me that feminism helps men too. By engaging with boys in an attempt to end violence against women, I was not only trying to make the world better for women but also for men. The issues surrounding feminism aren't solely female issues. As Tyler had taught me, they are human issues that impact us all.

CHAPTER ELEVEN
You can't make this stuff up!

"You have brains in your head and feet in your shoes. You can steer yourself in any direction you choose."

—Dr. Seuss

"What's pornography?"

Let's set the scene. I was in an eighth-grade class discussing sexual harassment and all things related to it. Specifically, we were talking about "sexting," which is the sending of sexually-provocative pictures via text message. The pornography subject arose when we broached what can happen when someone is caught with nude pictures of a person who is under the age of eighteen years old. An eighth-grade girl had just asked this question in response to the "you can be charged with the possession of child pornography" answer.

The lovely and talented teacher I was working with that day decided to field this question. I immediately thought two things when Ms. Thomas interjected with her answer.

Thank you!

This poor naïve student is about to have her world shaken up a little bit.

It's important to mention I was working in a Catholic school, and Ms. Thomas always did her best to attach as much of the program content to the religious teachings of the school.

"Well, class," Ms. Thomas began in a very uncertain tone, "pornography is when two people love each other very much."

What? It is? Did I need to check my notes on this? I wasn't sure where Ms. Thomas was going with this, and as I watched her, I started to realize *she* also didn't know where she was headed.

"When those two people love each other, they want to express that love in …" Ms. Thomas suddenly stopped.

I had hoped she would keep going because I desperately wanted to hear the end of this revolutionary pornography definition. Ms. Thomas closed her eyes for a second. It was like she was hoping the rest of the definition would appear to her. She opened her mouth again, but nothing came out. She then smiled sweetly and gave a half-hearted laugh.

"So two people love each other very much and …" Ms. Thomas's words hung in the air. "You know what? Never mind."

That was it—definition over.

I have been lucky enough to see life-changing moments in my job. I've witnessed courageous children discover new things about themselves, their lives, and the world around them, and I will never forget those moments. But I will also never forget the hilarious, awkward, and bizarre things I've seen in over a decade of classroom-based, social justice education. Ms. Thomas was one of those examples, but there are so many more. Many of those stories are as awkward and embarrassing to the teachers as they are to the students and me.

"Penis … Vagina … Intercourse."

That was the introduction done by a high school teacher prior to our healthy sexuality lesson. Before I even began, he did that little introduction, which was followed immediately by:

"Today, Travis is going to discuss sexuality with you. This doesn't have to be awkward or uncomfortable," the teacher continued.

"But sir, thanks to you, it already is," a student interjected.

"Well, let's try to be as open and honest as we can about this, and for you guys, let's try to last longer for this than you normally do," chuckled the teacher. "Does everyone think we can do that?"

One student's hand shot up immediately. "We can be mature and serious, sir," the student said.

"That's wonderful, Mia," the teacher responded.

"As long as you promise you won't speak for the rest of class," Mia answered.

The teacher laughed and shared a look with everyone that communicated how happy he was with that compromise. There was no question he was the one who was most uncomfortable with the day's topic.

But it wasn't always sex that initiated bizarre and amusing things to occur. The simplest thing in class can go terribly off track. When a student raises their hand, I just don't know what is going to happen. I *hope* what they are going to say is on topic. I *hope* it will somehow bring clarity to the minds of all their classmates with regards to the day's lesson. Most of all, I hope I can keep a straight face as they say it. Here is an example of a series on connections some fifth-grade students made.

"Can anyone tell me if the statement on the screen is an example of a stereotype or prejudice?" I asked my wide-eyed nine- and ten-year-olds.

A hand shot up with the confidence and conviction reserved for someone who knows exactly what I was talking about.

"My dad has a beagle. I really like him, but I can't pet him because he might bite me."

Now what do you do with that? How do you get back to the topic without dismissing the thoughts of a wonderfully sweet nine-year-old girl? Just then, another hand went up. I remember thinking, "Perfect, one of her classmates will bridge the gap and get us back on topic."

"I have a connection."

This seemed promising. When a student uses that phrase, it's usually a sign the lesson is having the desired effect.

"I have a beagle at home too. But it doesn't bite. I have to blow in it to make it do anything."

I stood there unsure of how this could possibly be a connection to *anything*. Then a light bulb went off and I realized she wasn't talking about a beagle but a *bugle.* She had a connection (even though it wasn't an accurate connection) to the previous statement, not to my lesson.

Before getting the chance to compose myself, and before I could acknowledge it, a little boy named Quinn said, "I have three things I need to share."

What the hell—it couldn't get worse, could it?

"Go ahead, Quinn."

"First, I don't like dogs because you have to pick up their poop. Second, I don't like cats because you have to scoop up their poop, and I think that's even worse."

I felt the urge to finally put a stop to the sharing session. I knew I needed to gain control of the conversation immediately if I had any hope of accomplishing anything during the lesson.

I interjected with, "Okay … thanks, Quinn. I understand what you're saying."

"I'm not finished. I said I had three things," Quinn replied.

Damn, I thought he wouldn't remember.

"Okay, Quinn, what else would you like to share?" I said wearily.

"Just that the answer was prejudice (he pronounces it pree-jew-dice). Isn't that what causes countries to have wars?"

And we were back. How we got back and how we made this unbelievable circuit from dogs to horns to poop and back again, I don't know. But this is the joy and pain of teaching social justice to nine-year-olds. Really, it's the joy more than anything. After all, Quinn made the connection between prejudice and global conflict. How many *adults* can do that?

I believe people need some inherent qualities to work well with children. I think you need to be open, honest, and see the best in every student. When you're working with children, these things can serve you well, but sometimes those traits can also backfire. Then, before you know it, you're quietly exiting the girls change room hoping no one has seen you.

As with most of my most bizarre moments, it all started with a boys group. For this particular group, we were confined to a little room that wasn't much bigger than a broom closet. I actually think it was a converted janitor's closet. It was a hot, muggy afternoon in May, and the boys were sweating. It's hard to describe the smell of sitting in such close quarters with eight twelve-year-old boys. It's a combination of body odor and Axe body spray that will never be made into a top-selling room deodorizer. Everyone in that little closet was hoping we could leave the room as soon as possible. Luckily, I had been given permission to use the school stage if we had an activity which required us to move around. Considering the smell and heat in that little room, I decided every activity we were going to do that day would require moving to the stage.

The boys and I went on a little road trip. We left the not-so-friendly confines of our dungeon-like room and went down the hall to the gym and onto the stage. We closed the curtain since there was a class using the gym and we wanted some privacy. The stage proved to be an excellent location for our activities. We did some communication exercises with blindfolds and tossed the ball around as we discussed what we had learned. The location was a nice break from the sweltering heat, but it was time to head back to the room and wrap up for the day. I didn't really want to interrupt the gym class that was in the middle of a basketball game, so I decided we would wait until there was a break in the action. Not so surprisingly, the guys didn't want to wait.

"Hey, Travis, I know a shortcut back to our room," said Ethan.

You'd think I would ask for some details when a twelve-year-old boy tells me they know a shortcut . You'd think I'd wonder how he knew about this shortcut and if he was, in fact, *supposed* to know about it. But not me. Nope.

"Great, let's go," I said and blindly followed Ethan and the rest of the boys down the stage stairs and into a narrow corridor. We walked down this hallway and up four or five steps before going through a doorway that led into an open space. It was dark, but I was able to make out some of the objects in the room. There were benches, what looked like some lockers, and some sinks. This is when I began to rethink what we were doing. I began to get a sinking feeling as we walked through the space.

"Guys? What exactly is this room?" I asked, fearing the answer.

"It's the girls' change room. We come through here all the time," Ethan answered like it was the most natural thing in the world.

I want to stress that thankfully, we were the only people in the change room. But I still felt like alarm bells were going off around the school. I could see the headline: "Violence Prevention Educator Teaches

Boys how to Sneak into the Girls' Change Room." Even if that headline wasn't true, the facts wouldn't paint me in a much better light. "Youth Educator Blindly Follows Boys into the Girls' Change Room."

Luckily, when we emerged from the change room and entered the hallway beside our little meeting room, classes were in session and no one was there to see us. I breathed a sigh of relief and quickly adjusted our group's topics to cover sexual harassment and boundaries.

Boys groups often provided me with the best stories I could share with my co-workers. Like the time I learned about the braiding skills of one of my participants. I was just in the opening stages of a boys group and we were playing a game called "Two Truths and a Lie." In this game, the guys are asked to share two true things about themselves and make up one lie. The rest of the group then tries to guess what is true so they can learn some new things about each other. I usually open the game so they get an idea of what will work well and make the game fun.

"I play hockey four times a week, I ran over and killed my cat, and I have a Superman tattoo," I shared with the group.

The boys all began to guess at once with the consensus being my tattoo was the lie.

"Sorry, guys, you're wrong. I do have a Superman tattoo on my left shoulder," I explained.

Not surprisingly, the boys didn't believe me.

"There is no way. You have to show us!" shouted an enthusiastic member named Alessandro.

This was not a shock to me because this often happened, so I confidently rolled up my sleeve and showed off my ink. This always seemed to help my credibility and usually got the boys groups off to a good start. My sharing usually encouraged the other guys to think up some creative things to share when it was their turn.

"I have a pet pig, I travel to Italy every summer, and my armpit hair is so long I can braid it," Alessandro announced when it was his turn.

The boys and I all took turns making our guesses. The Italy clue wasn't too hard to correctly identify as true since his name was Alessandro. But people did seem torn between the pet pig and armpit hair.

"I don't have a pet pig, but I do want one," said Alessandro.

"That means you really can braid your armpit hair?" asked another boy.

"Yeah, it's crazy long," said one of Alessandro's friends.

"Well, since I had to show my tattoo, I guess that means you need to show off your braiding skills, Alessandro," I replied.

Thus began my armpit hair-braiding tutorial. Guys hooted and hollered as Alessandro rolled up his t-shirt to reveal some of the longest hair I've ever seen. He then proceeded to carefully braid the hair and even topped it off with a bright-green hair tie. I can't imagine what that would have looked like from the outside because, even from the inside, it was pretty bizarre.

But to be fair, the boys' stories weren't always bizarre, funny, or creepy (like that last one). Sometimes they were sweet. I had one group of sixth-grade boys that challenged every male stereotype I knew. A great example of their openness and comfort was during a boundary exercise I often did in groups. The objective was to show how to set boundaries and what happens when they are violated. The example we chose that day was physical boundaries. I stood about fifteen feet away from one of the boys.

"Okay, Kevin, I'm going to slowly walk toward you. When you start to feel uncomfortable, simply tell me to stop. That will be an example of setting a boundary," I explained.

Usually, when I did this activity, the guys would stop me after six or seven steps. Sometimes, if they were really comfortable, they would let me get within a couple feet, but never any closer. I expected the same response from Kevin. I slowly began to walk toward him. I got up to about ten steps when I began to wonder, "Is he going to stop me?" As I kept walking forward, Kevin got a huge grin on his face. When I finally got about a foot away from him, he opened his arms and gave me a massive hug!

He looked at me and said, "If that's too close, Travis, just say stop to set your boundary."

POSTSCRIPT:

I have been lucky enough to work with young people for over ten years. It still amazes me how they can change my mood almost instantly. I can be having the worst day, and before I know what's happened, I've completely forgotten my troubles. Sometimes it's because the student's troubles are much more important than mine. But more often than that, it's because the energy and enthusiasm they bring to life each day is contagious. The young people I have worked with have made it impossible for me not to smile, laugh, and remember every day is a new chance for something amazing to happen.

CHAPTER TWELVE

Keeping It Real

"Education is the most powerful weapon which you can use to change the world."

—Nelson Mandela

My first five years in the VAW field taught me a lot. I had come a long way from my first few weeks and months on the job. Those initial days had been filled with uncertainty and trepidation as I tried to navigate a new role in a completely different atmosphere, all while wrestling with the question posed to me by Phyllis many years before.

"So … are you a feminist?"

I certainly was feeling more confident in my answer from a work and professional point of view. I knew my job had challenged my perspectives and made me consider things I had never thought of previously. I also knew I was proud of who I worked for and what I did, and I truly believed the work I did was important. But I couldn't say the job had impacted my personal life. I couldn't say it had inherently changed who I was. So, if I had been asked to answer Phyllis again, I still would have been a little uncertain.

Could I be a feminist at work and really not have it impact me at home? Was feminism what you did and what you believed in? Or was it more about who you were? If it was about who you were, I would have said I probably wasn't a feminist. I felt I was exactly the same guy I had been before I started in my VAW role. Yes, I understood things differently, but I was essentially the same person who had walked into an all-female environment five years earlier.

In reality, that wasn't true—I *was* different. Soon, I would come to realize it would be impossible *not* to be changed by the issues I was speaking about with such passion and conviction. As a result, it translated into doing things differently in my life too; I just hadn't realized it yet. Some of the strongest evidence of the fact I had changed actually lived with me.

Without even realizing it, I had a feminist living in my home. She just happened to be seven-years-old at the time. Somehow, what I learned had helped me raise a strong, independent daughter who had a very solid set of beliefs about the world around her. Even at the tender age of seven, Katie wasn't afraid to share her opinions or express her thoughts on what she felt were the pressing issues of the day. I still remember Katie sitting in the back of the car listening to the radio and sharing her thoughts on the day's hits.

"Dad, why does Beyoncé talk about putting a ring on *it*? Girls aren't 'it.'"

Or

"Dad, I really liked Selena Gomez before she took off all her clothes to sing."

I thought it was remarkable, and I was proud when I heard my daughter say these things. Honestly, sometimes I just wanted to listen to music without the critical thinking being broadcast from the backseat. But you reap what you sow, and I was glad to reap the benefits of having such a socially-conscious daughter.

Katie's awareness was often heard throughout the year, but it was often highlighted at Halloween through her costume choices. No fairy tale princesses or kitty cat costume for Katie. No, she chose strong female characters. Hermione Granger from the *Harry Potter* series, Katniss Everdeen from *The Hunger Games*, and Super Girl were a few of her choices. My daughter had even learned how to stand up for herself in a strong and respectful manner. One night, when we had some friends and their children over for dinner, an argument broke out amongst the kids. We heard raised voices and went upstairs to investigate.

"I feel upset when my toys get broken. I want my toys to be taken care of," Katie said.

"Whoa, did your seven-year-old just use an 'I' statement?" asked one of the moms.

Apparently, she had, and it worked like a charm.

Looking back, I can now conclude my parenting style was being impacted by what I was learning in my new role because it was obviously being passed on to my daughter. But I had no idea how much the journey into feminism and the world of violence against women had impacted me. Those discoveries would come through other areas of my life, shedding new light on things I hadn't viewed that way before.

Baseball had always been a big part of my life. I played it for years and had been playing on the same men's team for many years before I started my new job. The team was made up of a good group of guys. They were family men who came out to play hard, have fun, and have a beer before heading home. Our team was quite good and often competed for the top few spots in our league, but we were even more focused on having a good time—usually at each other's expense. It was not uncommon to hear things like:

"You're supposed to hit the ball with your bat, not your uterus!"

"You slid into second base like you were trying to protect your baby."

We all laughed and had a good time. Little thought was ever given to what the jokes meant. It was a slow progression for me to take what I was experiencing at work and translate it to my baseball games. I began to notice I felt a little less comfortable laughing when I heard some of those things. I still laughed, but it was becoming more about being accepted than truly seeing the humor in those statements. It reminded me of the boys groups and how many of those guys did the exact same thing. I wasn't sure about where my discomfort was coming from at first. Over time, I started to understand the disconnect between what I said at work and what I laughed at in the evening. I thought about something I often said to my students.

"How can we ever see someone as equal if they are the punch lines to our jokes?"

How could I ever say those things at work and expect people to live by them if I didn't live by them myself? It was during our next game that I worked up the courage to say something.

The game was a blowout, and when that happens, the joking and ribbing become heightened. One of our players went down looking at a third strike. When this occurs, there are often chants of "beer" and "he's buying the next round." Since it was a hot and muggy night, we were all looking forward to our free drink. But as Jay walked back to the dugout, another comment was thrown out by a guy next to me on the bench.

"Hey, Jay, maybe next week you can bring your wife's dress since you hit like a woman."

Every instinct I had wanted me to laugh and smile and keep my comments to myself, but another part of me felt something had to be said.

"I've seen Jay's wife hit. If we could all hit like her, maybe we'd win some more games."

It wasn't a complete condemnation of the comment. I know it didn't send the message that I felt the joke was sexist, but it felt like a way I could try to balance the scales a little bit. It was a start, and that start made it easier for me to say stronger things in the future. My teammates saw the change and were more careful with what they said around me. Once, when one of my teammates said something sexist, he said, "Sorry, Travis, I know you don't like stuff like that." It didn't mean the guys stopped saying those things altogether, but they did stop when I was around. I like to think it also gave them something to think about even when I wasn't there.

Coaching was another area in which I saw the shift in my attitude and behavior. This seemed to be more of a conscious change since I was in charge of the team. Now that I worked with children professionally, I felt I needed to coach my players the same way I taught the students in my classes. That can be difficult when you are coaching baseball with seven- and eight-year-olds. As is often the case, there were players sitting on the bases, looking in the opposite direction, and—my personal favorite—building sandcastles in the infield. Talk to any Pee Wee coach and they'll tell you, "That's life in the little leagues." An organized sport for children is often the definition of organized chaos, so you can't take it too seriously. I didn't think I took it too seriously. I had a very simple agenda I communicated to my players and their parents.

1. Have fun.
2. Learn to play baseball.
3. Be a good teammate.
4. Be a good opponent.
5. Try to improve your skills as a player and as a team.

I believed in this agenda. Like most people, I liked to win games, but if you make winning the focus of children's sports, I think you are destined for trouble. Sports are an incredible opportunity for character development and for the teaching of life skills. But sports can also bring out the worst in people if our priorities get mixed up. I would learn this during my first year coaching baseball.

That season, we had a wonderful group of players and parents. The players focused on improving, having fun, and on the butterflies that often fluttered about in the outfield. It wasn't an uncommon sight to see all our outfielders turned in the opposite direction watching the scenery instead of the game. For the most part, the other teams were positive and enjoyable opponents with children and parents who were simply enjoying the summer too. However, there were a few parents who saw things a little differently than I did. Their focus was on their children being the best and winning as often as possible. Sometimes, that created some tension. There were some discussions around rules, fair play, and how to celebrate in a way that was fair to the other team.

Our players were quite upset after one game when the opposing players said things like "too bad" and "you suck" during the postgame handshake instead of "good game." It was becoming clear to me that working with my team wasn't any different from the classroom. It was still about healthy relationships, managing emotions, and how to deal with things that sometimes seem unjust or unfair. We were all learning together, but I didn't know the biggest lesson of all was still to come, and it would be directed at me.

It happened on the last weekend of the season in the championship game. We were playing against the best team in our league by a wide margin. They also had the best player. Our team was playing their best baseball of the season. There were diving catches, big pitches, and timely hits on both sides, and it all made for a very exciting game. Both teams were having a great time playing in a big game that was so close. The game went back and forth with the lead changing hands many times. Finally, the other team gained control for good in the second-to-last inning.

It was then the mood began to change. The best player on the other team stepped to the plate with the bases loaded and his team comfortably ahead. He got hold of a pitch and crushed it to the outfield. Off the bat, I thought he could slowly jog around the bases and make it home without a throw even coming in. But before I knew it, one of our outfielders hustled back to grab the ball and started the relay to home plate. Meanwhile, the batter was running full speed around the bases. His dad was coaching third and frantically waved him toward home. It looked like it was going to be a close play. The ball reached the plate at almost the same time as the runner touched home, but the catcher never tagged the runner, which was required for him to be called "out."

By all logical reasoning, the best player in the league had hit an epic and very exciting grand slam home run in the final game of the season! But the umpire didn't see it the same way. In fact, the umpire seemed very nervous and unsure about the call. A few seconds seemed to go by before she very cautiously, and without any confidence, signaled the runner was "out."

Everyone was a little shocked, and things seemed to grind to halt as the entire diamond went silent. That is, until we all heard a loud bark coming from third base. The father of the player yelled, "What? You have to be crazy!" and began to walk very quickly toward the umpire. Before anyone knew what was happening, he was screaming in the umpire's face that she had gotten the call wrong. The umpire was obviously shaken. As a sixteen-year-old, she was getting experience umpiring the younger children's games and seemed unprepared for any type of conflict.

The scene playing out in front of me was of an adult man screaming in the face of a sixteen-year-old girl in front of a group of kids who were playing the game of their young lives. I've thought a lot about what happened next and why I got involved. The only explanation I have is, my new job had a deeper impact on me than I had realized. I'd seen arguments and unjust things before and honestly felt badly about them, but I never saw it as my responsibility to intervene. As if on autopilot, I walked onto the diamond and got between the umpire and the father. Without thinking, I was nose-to-nose with this guy yelling at him as vigorously as he had been yelling at the umpire. My argument wasn't about the call because it was obviously wrong. My argument was about how he was handling it.

In no uncertain terms, I told him his son was "safe" and the run would count. I then told him he had to go sit down and stop intimidating the umpire. My entire tirade took less than a minute, but it would stay with me for ages. I felt good about standing up for someone; it was the right thing to do. *How* I'd done it had exacerbated an already volatile situation though.

It didn't matter that the man I confronted had been aggressive and difficult all year. It didn't matter that the parents applauded as I left the diamond. It didn't even matter that the umpire would thank me a year later when I was in her high school class. What *did* matter was that I was supposed to be a role model for my players and for the kids I teach in class. I teach assertive communication and managing anger and had failed to do either of those things in a stressful situation.

That day, I learned my job and all the stories I was exposed to had changed me at my core. I now had a stronger sense of what was right and wrong, and as a result, would react more quickly when I saw something unjust. But I also realized I hadn't learned enough yet. I needed to incorporate what I taught the children in my classes more fully into my life. After all, children won't listen to your words as much as they will follow your example. When I thought back to *why* I started in my new job, I remembered I wanted to do something important and something that made a difference. I now knew the only way I could truly accomplish that was to ensure I practiced what I preached. To teach it, I had to live it in the classroom, at home, and in whatever other interests I pursued—including playing and coaching sports.

The world of sports has created some of the most inspirational stories ever told. Books, movies, YouTube videos, and personal recollections often center around someone doing something amazing in sports. Often, it is an awesome athletic performance, but just as often it's about someone's perseverance, kindness, and integrity in sports. Sadly, sports also can show us the dark side of our society. There have been countless stories about professional athletes cheating, getting in trouble with the law, and even abusing their loved ones. I think we can use sports as a vehicle to teach positive character traits and improve the world around us. I have learned that through my own sports experiences. The locker room banter, the emotional reactions, and the ability to deal with failure and difficult situations are all training opportunities.

I hoped to use these things in the years ahead, both in my school programs and my coaching opportunities. What I didn't know at the time was there was about to be a whole new venue in which I could explore and practice these things, and it would push me in ways I couldn't imagine.

CHAPTER THIRTEEN
MENtors

"Change will not come if we wait for some other person or for some other time."

—Barack Obama

The agency I worked for had broken new ground when they hired me. They had taken the unique approach of hiring a man to help send the message that violence against women was an important issue which needed to be addressed. My hiring had raised more than a few eyebrows and had started a conversation about how to engage more men in addressing the issue of gender-based violence. It was a conversation that had its proponents and its detractors. Some felt women had worked so hard for so long to bring attention to the VAW issue that it was a disservice to those women to bring in men to "save the day." But my agency wasn't looking for men to "save the day." They were simply looking for men to add their voices to the women who had been speaking about the issue so passionately for generations. With that in mind, my workplace continued down the path of engaging even more men. They attracted and added men to their board of directors and even took the unheard-of step of electing a male to serve as the president of that board. Finally, the board decided they would support a committee of volunteer men from the community to begin long-term discussions about men's engagement.

Naturally, as the only male employee of my agency, I wanted to be a part of this committee. It was with all this lead-up that I found myself sitting in the agency boardroom with six other men at the first meeting of our men's engagement committee. I still remember each of us looking at each other, and the looks all seemed to say the same thing: "Okay, now what?" The men who sat around the table that night all had some sort of connection to the agency. They either served, or had served, on the board of directors, had done some sort of contract work for the organization, or, as in my case, were employed there full-time. But even with that connection, there still seemed to be confusion on how to start. The goal of the group, while not specifically spelled out at that time, was pretty simple to understand: engage men in helping to reduce and eliminate violence against women in our community. But, as I had learned during my time working in the VAW field, "simple to understand" and "easy to accomplish" were two very different things. How could we engage men? Where could we start? What should we do? It was the last question that seemed to get the most attention.

As is often the case with men, we wanted to *do* something, so we began with an action. When I look back now on that first meeting, I laugh a little. We were so eager to get started and make a difference! We all felt we needed something tangible to come out of that first meeting, and while created a great initiative, something was missed that night. In our eagerness to get started, we didn't take the time to truly understand the issues surrounding violence against women. At this time, I had been working in my job for over five years, and I still could honestly say I didn't understand all the issues. After ten years, I still know I don't fully comprehend everything that contributes to systemic violence against women. Yet, that night, we all felt confident enough to proceed with our first campaign. Our hearts were in the right place, but our perspective couldn't possibly be. We didn't even know what we didn't know yet. That would come back to haunt us, but at that moment, it was full speed ahead!

With all of that said, our first activity was extremely successful. It was a poster campaign designed to capture real fathers from the community posing with their daughters. We chose local athletes, police officers, school representatives, and businessmen. The posters were designed to send the message that these men supported their daughters' rights to a violence-free future. The positive response to the poster campaign quickly propelled it into a second set of posters. This time, the posters showed local men who worked with groups of boys within the community. We had teachers, coaches, fathers with sons, and the local police foundations class pose for posters. The purpose this time was to show positive male role models in action as they taught young boys what it really meant to be men. The posters began to gain so much positive traction for the group that the committee began to grow. Before we knew it, we had twelve men sitting around the table discussing other ways we could engage men in conversations about violence against women.

It was interesting for me to see so many other men starting to become involved with my organization. It made me wonder what their motivation was for joining our committee. Could it be as simple as being inspired by the posters? Were the pictures and messages *that* compelling? Or did the posters simply trigger something that was already there for these men?

I quickly learned each of these men had their own motivating factors for being a part of the group. The poster campaign and creation of the men's engagement committee finally gave them an outlet where they could express things they had been thinking for a long time. In fact, listening to the reasons and conversations surrounding everyone's involvement became my favorite part about being a member of this group. I got a chance to hear everyone's story. Whether it was as a part of a group discussion or by getting to know the guys personally, I began to understand the many different reasons a man had for joining the group.

From my experience, I realized their involvement could be broken down into two distinct motivating factors. The first reason was many of the men had known a woman who had experienced some form of violence committed against her at some point in her life. Some stories were personal, and some were from the workplace, but all of them had left an indelible impression on each of the men. Much like me with the school-based stories, each of them had experienced violence against women differently once they could put a face to it.

I also had a strong connection to the second motivating factor that brought many of these men to our committee. They had daughters. When you hear and truly believe more than half of Canadian women will experience violence in their lifetime, it changes you. It changes you even more when you have a daughter. It's hard to fathom your daughter has a better chance of being a victim of violence than living a life free of violence. But once you realize it's true, your perspective permanently changes.

That perspective shift was the most important reason I had become so passionate about my job and now my volunteer opportunity. I had a daughter and wanted to do whatever I could to make the community she was living in safer for her. That was also the biggest reason the group had grown. It made me start to wonder if I would still be doing this job if my daughter had been born a son. If I were being honest, the answer would probably be "no." I likely wouldn't see the issues the same way if I were raising a boy.

That realization filled me with a great feeling of shame. It made me feel like my entire reason for being a part of VAW work was selfish and inauthentic. The truth was, if I were raising a son, it would be even *more* important for me to be involved in this work. I'm thankful for my daughter for many reasons, but one of the biggest reasons is, she got me here. Yes, my motivations for trying to promote gender equality and prevent gender-based violence may be a little self-serving since I have a daughter, but *because* I have a daughter, I now understand that. I also understand if I had a son, I would need to find a way for him to understand that too. We need both genders working together to truly address the issues surrounding VAW. That's why I have come to believe so strongly in the men's engagement initiative. We have stumbled and had a few missteps, but we're still at the table, and we're still having the conversations.

A lot of work has been done to empower girls and women in our society. As a parent raising a daughter, I celebrate and love the different messages, programs and initiatives created to help girls understand they are worthwhile, important, and powerful. We need a generation of girls to help lead our society toward true gender equality and away from misogyny. But isn't it just as important to empower boys? That may sound bizarre since men having power is a large part of the problem. But what if we could *re*-empower boys? What if we could show them power doesn't have to be associated with domination? What if it were possible to teach boys that compassion and empathy are the largest forms of strength attainable? What if we could have a generation of boys work alongside the girls to create a culture built on acceptance and equality?

My committee's hope was that we could begin to start down that path by engaging like-minded fathers of both daughters and sons. We would try to do that many ways in the years to come. Through that work, we would learn what we are capable of and what our limitations were.

CHAPTER FOURTEEN
The Many Faces of Women

"Feminism isn't about making women stronger. Women are already strong. It's about changing the way that the world perceives that strength."

—G.D. Anderson

For a man trying to walk in a woman's shoes, it's amazing to consider all the time I had spent working with boys and men during my time in an all-female agency. The boys groups, the dads program, and even MENtors had become a large part of my career in the VAW sector. I still had had the opportunity to work with girls and women on a regular basis. Through co-ed classrooms, the all-female health classes, those postpartum groups, and interacting with my co-workers every day, I had been provided with many amazing stories to share.

One of the most memorable women was a teenager named Kathy. Kathy was a loud, outspoken "firecracker" of a person I first met in an alternative education class conducted by a local high school. The first time I encountered her was when she burst into the classroom like a tsunami. Based on the reaction, it seemed everyone had been waiting for Kathy's arrival.

"What's up, bitches!" Kathy yelled as she entered the room.

"Hey, Kathy, you look really nice. What are you all dressed up for?" asked one of the students.

"You gotta look nice if you're gonna work the street corner!" Kathy replied.

I was prepared for a different environment when I worked in "alt. ed." These were students who had struggled in a regular classroom setting and were earning their high school credits off-campus in a local community center. The atmosphere was intentionally much more laidback and less rigid. The students were able to do their schoolwork on couches instead of at desks, the start and end times were much more flexible, and as a result, the students often felt more comfortable to be themselves. Colorful language and crude jokes weren't very shocking, but Kathy took it to another level. She never held back, even when it was at my expense.

I will never forget the time I arrived to do my weekly session with the students and found them doing yoga. The lights had been dimmed, and there was soft music playing as all the students were stretched out in a variety of yoga poses. I tried to quietly enter the room so I wouldn't disrupt the mood. As it turned out, I didn't have to worry too much about disrupting anything because Kathy was in the class. I went about attempting to set down my things quietly and tried to go unnoticed. It was at that point Kathy went on an epic yoga-hating rant.

"Oh my God, I think I just split my pants. This sucks, Mrs. W. I'm going to kill you for making me do this. Why do we have to do yoga anyway?"

Kathy took a breath and started up again.

"I'm no gymnast, you know. Oh, my back is killing me. Everyone can probably see my butt crack."

Just then, she noticed I was in the room.

"Oh God! Travis, get out! Seriously, *leave* the room now. This is embarrassing. Please go … and you better not be looking at my ass!"

Needless to say, I did her the favor of leaving the room until they were finished—and no, I wasn't looking at her ass.

But even with all Kathy's bluster and ferocity, I could tell she had a huge heart, along with a large social conscience. What I liked best about Kathy was, someone always knew what she thought and where they stood. That was very clear on the day we did a class activity called "Road to Romance." This game had been designed so the class could share what they thought the logical steps to an intimate relationship were. On the board, I posted twenty different cards; each had a different step toward sex. Some example cards were: eye contact, birth control, holding hands, kissing, talking, and hugging. There were two sets of cards, so two different groups of students could create their own "Road to Romance."

The students made their own groups—boys versus girls. Each group couldn't see the other's cards, so at the end, there would be a big reveal with each team sharing their road with the other. You might be able to guess how the two roads differed. The girls' road utilized most of the cards and started with talking. It also included hugging and kissing before doubling back to more talking. In fact, they used the talking card in four different spots. By contrast, the boys' road included a grand total of three cards.

1. Eye Contact
2. Birth Control
3. Intercourse

There were the predictable giggles and chuckles as the guys shared their road with the girls, but Kathy wasn't amused.

"You can't be serious. What, do you think if you look me in the eye and hold up a condom, I'm just going to come running?"

The boys seemed genuinely offended by the critique of their presentation.

"We were just joking. Chill out, Kathy."

She wasn't going to be appeased that easily. She asked the guys to show her what they thought the real road would look like. So the guys changed their road to include alcohol. You can imagine how that went over.

Thus began one of the best classes I've ever taught. And I did nothing. For forty minutes, the boys and girls debated the logical, healthy, and safe steps to an intimate relationship. It got heated at times, but it was incredible to watch. I simply sat back with the teacher and watched as Kathy held court. To their credit, the boys began to take it seriously and responded with equal intensity. At the end, the boys and girls met on some common ground and were able to laugh and reflect on what had just happened. All I could think was, "Thank you, Kathy!" It was inspiring to see such a strong and confident girl take a stand. If we could empower more girls and create more moments like this, our world would be so much better.

Another example of a strong girl came in the form of a ten-year-old named Tabbi. She was in a fifth-grade class where I was running an eight-lesson program on stereotypes. Tabbi was the epitome of an activist. She commented on everything. From bullying to empathy, she had an opinion. She often took center stage and spoke at length about her thoughts on the day's topic. The other students in the class seemed to have no trouble acquiescing to her. They seemed to enjoy listening to her as much as I did. Truth be told, I often felt I should give her a portion of my paycheck—she was that good.

Then came the day we discussed self-esteem. For this lesson, the students were split into four teams and asked to line up in front a flipchart. The goal of the activity was for the students to approach the flipchart paper one at a time and write something they liked about themselves. It was something I had done with great success many times before. It was always uplifting to see the students writing as much as they could while receiving encouragement from their peers. I put on some music, and the game began. I made my way around to each team, pausing to see what they were writing, but as I approached Tabbi's team, there seemed to be something wrong. The line wasn't moving, and she was standing at the front of the line.

"Tabbi doesn't know what to write," said one of the students as I approached.

I could hear the other students in line giving Tabbi ideas in rapid succession, but she just stood there frozen. The marker was in the air just above the paper, but it wasn't moving.

"Tabbi, do you need some help?" I asked as gently as I could.

Tears began to well up in her eyes. That was just before she bolted from the room. When I tracked her down, she was sitting on the floor against the wall of the hallway just outside the classroom.

"Tabbi, do you want to talk about what's bothering you?" I asked.

"I don't know the answer," she replied softly.

"Well, your classmates had a lot of ideas for you. Do you want to write down one of those things?"

"But you said it was supposed to be something that *you* liked about *yourself*," Tabbi said with great conviction. "I can't think of anything I like about myself," she continued. "I feel so fat all the time. I try to watch what I eat, but nothing helps. I'm disgusting!"

As it turned out, Tabbi had an eating disorder. She would often go to the bathroom after she ate and make herself vomit. Her outward presentation of self-assured confidence was masking some serious feelings of insecurity.

I will never forget that conversation as I thought to myself, "How can't you see how truly remarkable you are?"

Thankfully, Tabbi got the help she needed. She took some time off from school, and when she came back, she was a little less gregarious and outgoing. Over time, the spark slowly returned, but this time it was backed up by some genuine self-confidence. In fact, the next year I was in her class, she did a presentation on female representation in the media. She discussed makeup, Photoshop, body image issues, and eating disorders. It seemed she was going to use her experience to help others. Now *that* is strength.

Of all the women I have met during my travels, the most courageous ones are those who have lived where I work. They have been residents of our shelter. These are the women who have had the courage to leave their homes so they and their children could be safe. I can't imagine having to make that choice, but they did, and I've had the honor of listening as they tell their stories. I've listened to them speak at meetings and public events, and I'm always left in awe of how they survived and now have the courage to talk about it.

It always makes me think about who is living in our shelter right now. How difficult it must be to be hurt by someone you love and who is supposed to love you. It's why I completely understand when I cross paths with a female client in our building and see a specific look in her eye. The look I often see is fear. As the only male employee in my agency, some of our clients are surprised or a little taken aback when they see me walking around the building.. Those looks always fill me with great sadness and anger. I'm looked at with fear because of my gender and what some men have done. Of all the walks I have taken in a woman's shoes, the most powerful one is when I see a woman look at me and not see a man but a potential threat. Beyond my daughter, this is the thing that motivates me most to keep doing my job.

My experience has given me the chance to see firsthand the damage misogyny and gender-based violence can do. At the same time, I've also seen how much better our world can be when we have strong, healthy women helping to lead it—women and girls like Kathy and Tabbi. I can't imagine having to see either of them walk into our shelter one day. I want to work as hard as I can to make sure I never do.

CHAPTER FIFTEEN
December 6th

"The abuse of women and girls is the most pervasive and unaddressed human rights violation on earth."

—Former United States President Jimmy Carter

During my journey into feminism, I've had many moments of education—moments when things become clearer. Sometimes, those moments have been painful and difficult to learn from and bear witness to. Other times, I'm simply left speechless by the atrocities that lie beneath the surface of our society. December 6th is a day anyone associated with VAW work circles on their calendar. It's also become a day when the men I volunteer with make their presence most visible to the community.

December 6th, 1989 is the day violence against women in Canada gained national attention in the most horrific of ways. That morning, a man named Marc Lepine entered École Polytechnique de Montréal armed with a 223-caliber Sturm-Ruger rifle. Once inside the school, Lepine went into an engineering classroom and ordered the male students to leave while simultaneously telling the female students to move to the back of the room. In his attack on the school, Lepine very purposely targeted only the female engineering students stating, "You're all a bunch of feminists. I hate feminists."

In a note found later, Lepine blamed feminists for ruining his life. He went on to say women had no place in engineering because they would take away jobs from men. As a result of the attack, fourteen women were killed that day, followed shortly by Lepine as he took his own life.

I was sixteen years old in 1989. On the day of the attack at École Polytechnique de Montréal, I got up and went to school. Later, I went to work at my part-time job and returned home to catch the day's sports highlights. I had no idea about the horrifying events that had unfolded in Montréal. I was a naïve and self-centered teenager at the time. Beyond sports, school, my job, and the relationships in my life, I had little concept of the world around me. It was probably quite normal for most teens to be that unaware of current events in a world before Internet and social media. The hard thing for me to admit is, my lack of knowledge went well beyond my teenage years.

Almost two decades later, I became fully aware of what had occurred on that dark day in Canadian history. It took me joining a VAW organization to understand what the events of December 6th, 1989 truly meant. If I hadn't had the opportunity to walk in women's shoes, would December 6th still be just a regular day on the calendar for me? It also makes me contemplate how many people walk around each December 6th as unaware as I was.

I was officially introduced to December 6th through an annual vigil my organization hosts. Agency employees, local political figures, police officers, and community members come together in front of our shelter to remember the women who lost their lives that day in 1989. Remembering the fourteen women who died at École Polytechnique de Montréal would be moving and impactful all by itself. But the vigil goes beyond that by remembering *all* the women and children who have died in Canada as a result of domestic violence.

I remember my first vigil very clearly. It was a typical cold and gray December day in Ontario. The vigil is held outside, so I recall the cold bite on my nose and how my legs quickly went numb. Since I worked inside the building, I was outside earlier than most and saw the crowd slowly begin to form. As I looked at the large group assembled with candles in their hands, I was taken back to my first week on the job when I stood in a room full of women.

Beyond a police officer and a couple of other men scattered amongst the small crowd, the entire group was female. I remember thinking at the time how wrong it felt. Did most men not know about the vigil? Or did they all simply have more important things to do? I could understand the lack of male attendees a little. The truth was, I probably wouldn't think to come to an event like this if it weren't for my professional involvement in the cause. We live in a world that is busier than ever. People's work schedules are hectic, and their children seem to juggle more extracurricular activities. When you combine that with the plethora of worthwhile causes also requiring people's time and money, you can see why many events draw fewer people than they used to.

This was different though. This wasn't a fundraiser or a charity walk. It was a service to remember not only women in a city a province away two decades ago but also women who'd lost their lives in our community. These were women we knew or smiled at in the grocery store. They were women whose children attended the same schools our children did and worked in places we frequented every day. These thoughts all went through my mind as the service began.

As I look back on my first December 6th vigil, and the ones that have come since, it's hard to describe how I felt. That is interesting because I can recall specific feelings and details from most parts of my VAW work life. But this event is different. It's one of the reasons I've never spoken at the vigil. I've had the opportunity to speak, but I've always found a way out of it. It's not due to nerves or fear of public speaking. I've spoken to every group imaginable during my time in this job. On December 6th, I can never find the words to describe my feelings. How could I ever find the right thing to say to the group that assembles each year to remember those whom we have lost?

If I were pressed into describing my feelings during that first vigil, I would say … numb. Not just from the cold but also from the words I heard. It's one thing to hear statistics, but when you hear names and see faces, it makes it much more real. It was very similar to when I spoke with that high school student in my first few weeks on the job and she told me she had been sexually assaulted. Violence as a concept is disturbing. Violence as a reality is much more than that. As I listened to the names read aloud that day from Montréal and closer to home, I felt deep sadness, intense anger, and even shame. When I felt all these things at once, it was so overwhelming, I was left with a deep feeling of numbness. This feeling continued as we all tied white ribbons on the tree outside our shelter as a local woman sang "I Will Remember You" by Sarah McLachlan. It was in that moment I vowed to remember this day and why the work that was being done was so important.

What bothers me most about December 6th each year is, there are women from the most recent year whom we have to remember as well. A woman is killed *every 2.5 days* in Canada. So, while we continue to speak and take action, the violence continues year after year.

With that in mind, I was eager to join the men's engagement group when it was formed. We were originally called the Headwaters White Ribbon Campaign. This name was taken from the Toronto-based White Ribbon Campaign started by the late Jack Layton in response to the 1989 Montréal Massacre. It has since grown to become an international movement. It also seemed appropriate to me since one of my true "aha" moments came when I was hanging a white ribbon on our remembrance tree. Since that time, the group has changed and morphed a little, adopting the name MENtors for a little more clarity on what we do and who we are. It was this group that decided to take the December 6th vigil and try to turn it on its head.

"The day we need to make our presence felt most is December 6th," said Mike, our committee chairman.

There were no objections from the group. Instead, there was a palpable feeling of enthusiasm and excitement. I've learned the men's engagement group likes projects, just like at that first meeting when we decided to take on a poster campaign in our first five minutes of existence. The men on our committee feel they need to have something tangible to work on when they leave a meeting. They want to be action-based, which, in my opinion, is very admirable but can also lead to complications. For me, the discussions and deeper understanding the dialogue leads us to is the most important part of our meetings. For many of us, we want to know we are *doing* something when, in fact, discussing and understanding may be the most important thing we can be *doing*. But with that little preamble aside, the men's engagement committee decided to take a more active role in the December 6th Day of Remembrance.

Before this decision, we had simply shown up. We tried to balance the audience by having more men present. We tried to encourage our male friends, family members, and work colleagues to join us, and it had worked. Each year, there were more men standing shoulder to shoulder with the women as the candles were lit. We also had taken the step of having one of our committee members speak. There were some excellent speeches that called for other men to come forward and stand with us. So the question was, "What else could we do to really make a statement about men's engagement?"

"We need to be visible. We need to make a spectacle the community will notice," I suggested.

"What's more visible than a group of men marching to the vigil?" Mike responded. "Instead of just showing up, let's make everyone in town *know* we are showing up at the vigil," he continued.

At that point, the ideas started to come fast and furious.

"We should get as many men and boys as we can to march with us right down the main street to the vigil."

"Maybe we can get some male high school students involved."

"We should get some of the male police officers and even encourage the male members from town council to walk with us."

"We'll carry a banner out front so everyone knows what we are doing."

So that was it. We had this nailed down in about five minutes. Our concept was to have over a hundred men marching down the main street with a banner declaring we were opposed to violence against women. We would march right into the vigil as a group showing we supported all the women who had been coming to the vigil for decades. It sounded pretty good. To be honest, it sounded amazing. What could be better than creating a spectacle? People would know men were joining the cause. Not only would the community know about December 6th but they would learn about it from a bunch of like-minded men. There was no thought in my mind this would be viewed as anything but positive. What could the downside possibly be?

The downside was, we were looking at this from a man's point of view. I couldn't have imagined the difference in point of view could change our plan of support into a plan some people felt was inappropriate and insulting.

"With all due respect, guys, I think this idea may hurt more than it helps things."

The words hung in the air for a few moments. The men at the table were a little stunned and more than a little uncomfortable. It was like the air had been taken out of the balloon of excitement. No one spoke for a few seconds, and then slowly, they all turned their attention to the person who had burst the bubble. All the men listened to what the only woman in the room would say next.

"Your hearts are in the right place, but the time for this is not December 6th," said Judy.

Judy was my organization's representative on the men's engagement committee. While it's true I also worked for the same organization, I was volunteering. Judy sat on the committee as part of her job to ensure the organization was represented appropriately and to offer a female perspective. It seemed the time for that perspective was now.

As I look back, I remember feeling angry, confused, and defeated. I mean, if December 6th wasn't the time for a strong male statement, when *was* the time?

"Some of the women who come to this vigil have been coming here for over twenty years. They have stood here in the cold every year. They have sometimes stood with only a handful of others. Most times they stood with only women looking back at them. How do you think they might feel if a small army of men marches in?" Judy spoke with raw emotion in her voice.

I wanted to tell her the women should feel supported and like they were no longer alone. I wanted to yell and scream that the time for action was now. I felt like throwing up my hands and giving up.

"December 6th is about remembering those whom we have lost. It has to be a *somber* time for reflection," continued Judy. "My fear is, the headline in the paper on December 7th will be about a group of men marching, albeit for a good cause. But on December 6th, the story has to be about the women."

As quickly as the march was on, it was off. The impact of this meeting was devastating … but also necessary. Many of the men, including myself, felt frustrated, disillusioned, and even angry our attempt to send a message had been thwarted. But it was also a turning point for me and many of the other men on our committee. Up until then, almost all our time had been spent doing things. Poster campaigns, community breakfasts, service club presentations, and social media updates dominated most of our time, but now we had been stopped in our tracks. We had been forced to listen and reflect. We had to take the time necessary to try to better understand a woman's perspective.

When I took the time to do that, Judy's words suddenly made much more sense to me. I tried to imagine being a woman who had stood in solidarity with a very small group of like-minded women for decades. They had braved the cold and remembered the women we had lost when very few others had taken the time to do so. I thought of how I would feel if a group of men suddenly marched in with cameras flashing and the proverbial trumpets blaring. If I were one of those women, my response would have been very simple.

"Where the hell have you been?" and "What took you so long?"

I wasn't the only one who came to this conclusion. A few weeks later, we had a very emotional and productive meeting. The tone of the group had changed. There seemed to be less rush to take action and a desire for more discussion and understanding. It was clear if we wanted to be productive male allies, we would need to the take the time to develop empathy and understanding. We would need to put ourselves in a woman's shoes. It was decided the time for marching would come, but December 6th was not that time. Instead, we would once again simply be there and have one of our members speak. That day, the words spoken by one of our committee members captured our journey perfectly.

"My name is Don, and I am a proud member of the MENtors group. We are a group of men committed to ending violence against women. Today, I will be silent as we remember the women we have lost. During the remaining 364 days of the year, I will not be silent. I will speak out against gender-based violence in all of its forms. I encourage other men to do the same."

That was it. It was the shortest speech our group had ever spoken at the December 6th vigil, yet it said more than we had ever said before. December 6th wasn't a day for us to make noise. It was our day to be silent. But on every other day of the year, we would be anything but silent about the issue of violence against women. One way we would be less than silent would be by clomping down Main Street in our bright-pink high-heeled shoes.

CHAPTER SIXTEEN
A Walk in Her Shoes

"It is by standing up for the rights of girls and women that we truly measure up as men."

—Desmond Tutu

"He said he'd kill me if I left. But I knew eventually he'd kill me if I stayed."

Those words were spoken by a survivor of domestic violence, and they were powerful enough all by themselves. But something else that made the words special was the audience listening to them. The audience consisted of about fifty men. They were looking a little worse for wear as they stood, sat, and slumped nearby wearing their pink high-heeled shoes. It was the third annual MENtors Walk in Her Shoes event, and for the first time, we were hearing the words of a survivor. It meant we weren't only walking in a woman's shoes. We were also starting to truly understand *why* we needed to.

The Walk in Her Shoes event was the group's response to the December 6th idea for a march. Through some discussion and research, we decided to take the idea that had been used by several other communities and literally "walk in her shoes." The result was unbelievable. It's hard to describe what it's like to be surrounded by a group of men all wearing high heels. It's funny and more than a little weird, but it's also strangely empowering. To see a group of guys get together with the common goal of ending violence against women is amazing.

The learning curve for men who attempt to walk in high-heeled shoes is a steep one. Most of us go from size to size searching for a comfortable fit. It's only after we try on several different pairs do we realize these shoes weren't designed with comfort in mind. It always brings to mind a couple of important questions.

"How do women wear these things?"

"*Why* do women wear these things?"

Then there are the first few tentative steps. I imagine it looks similar to a child's first time on skates. God knows we sound like children trying to skate for the first time (oh, the whining). There are terrified looks, staggered attempts at walking while holding on to something, and warning shouts of "stay away!" Then, as men start to feel more comfortable, there are a few guys who start to show off. This is usually followed by comments like:

"You were born for this."

"All that practice at home seems to be paying off."

I always want to tell the first timers who are sprinting around to slow down. After three years of experience, I know the early walk adrenaline will soon be replaced by sore calves, blistered feet, and the odd broken shoe. But since experience is the best teacher, I keep my opinion to myself.

The minutes before the walk begins are some of my favorite moments. There is a nervous energy in the air. There is a lot of good-natured ribbing from fellow walkers toward each other. There are comments about each other's legs, our choice of socks (apparently, knee-high Superman socks are a fashion faux-pas), and about our lack of walking skills. Then there are the comments from our so-called supporters. These are the people who came with us. I often think if marathon runners had supporters like ours, no one would ever finish a race, but it's all in good fun. Then, there are the people who aren't connected to the walkers or the event who just happen to walk by as we get ready. I had never been catcalled or whistled at before I put on high heels, but I certainly have been while sporting the pink shoes. Sometimes, I feel like a model making the walk down the runway, especially with all the cameras going off. If there has ever been an event that doubled as a photo shoot, this would the one. There are pictures of grandfathers with granddaughters, brothers and sisters, husbands and wives, and of course, fathers with their daughters. The photo's I've taken at this event are some of my favorites. It's very inspiring to watch it all unfold in the name of ending violence.

The walk itself has evolved over the years. We started at only about 200 feet on a paved path by a hockey arena. But now, three years later, we finally got the march we first envisioned. It takes us down the main street of our town and lasts for several blocks (be careful what you wish for). I must say, I wasn't prepared for the reaction from the onlookers when we march in our high-heeled shoes. It's gratifying and more than a little humbling.

Besides the good-natured heckling and whistles, we also get something else as we walk by the local shops and restaurants. We get applause. It was something I never expected, and it's difficult to know how to respond to it, but it happens without fail every time we pass a populated area. Word slowly spreads we are coming, and we see people start to emerge from the shop or store we are passing. There are looks of bewilderment, smiles, and without exception, cheers. Even more startling are some of the things people have said as we walk by. There are the obvious things like "good job, guys," but then there are other comments that, quite frankly, leave me speechless.

"Thank you for walking!"

"What a cool thing you guys are doing."

"This is so inspiring to see!"

It's the "thank yous" that get to me. These happen during the walk, and after we are finished, women I've never met before come up and thank me personally. I'll never forget the time two women stopped a small group of walkers I was with.

"I just want you to know I currently live in the women's shelter in town. Seeing you guys do this is amazing, and it gives me hope. I just wanted to thank you," said one of the women.

Her words hung in the air for a moment or two. Each of the men looked at each other and back to her as she stood there holding her young son's hand. It was clear we had no idea how to respond.

"You're welcome" seemed completely inappropriate. It would have felt condescending and like we had done her some sort of favor. But we also knew saying nothing would be equally wrong. I kept thinking, "Where is my feminist friend Phyllis when I need her?" She would know what to say.

Just as I was thinking that, one of the guys spoke up. "Well, we think it's the right thing to do."

It was simple, but it was also an acknowledgment of her appreciation and, most importantly stated, we felt it was our responsibility. To me, it summed up things perfectly. Then, just as we turned to go, we heard a small voice.

"Can I try?"

Her son wanted to try out the high-heeled shoes. To say he put us to shame is putting it mildly. He ripped around in shoes six sizes too big for him like he was born for them. It made me think the next generation could be different and things could get better through experiences like this one. Since then, we've had quite a few "junior" walkers. They often walk with their fathers, sometimes with their mothers, and they always do it faster and easier than everyone else. It makes me wonder if their acceptance of an equal and non-violent culture might also come easier than it has for my generation.

Another thing I noticed was, we were getting regular audience members. These supporters not only joined us at the high-heeled shoes walk but also anytime the men's group appeared at a local event. They were the supporters of the agency I work for and had become supporters of ours as well. It gave me great comfort when I spoke publicly to be able to see so many friendly faces and people I knew were in our corner. There was one woman who began to stand out to me. She often stood on the outskirts of the crowd nodding and smiling as I or another member of my group spoke. She was so reliable, I even began to look for her when I spoke at events. One day, without me realizing it, this woman was standing beside me.

She smiled, put her hand on my arm, and very quietly said, "I want you to know I think you are the answer."

It was so quiet and so quick, I wasn't sure I had heard her correctly. Before I could process what she had said, she was gone. It happened again a few months later. The woman was like a supportive ninja suddenly appearing with some words of encouragement and then gone just as quickly. It became a regular occurrence and always included some variation of "I think you are the solution or answer."

I began to think about what was truly being said. After all, I wanted to be able to respond to her one of these times. I wanted to have something to say instead of dumbly muttering "thank you." After years of attending VAW events like vigils, fundraisers, and rallies, this woman was getting hope from our little group of men. For this woman to see men sending the message they were opposed to violence, it showed her things could get better. It showed her things could change because, in some small way, they already had.

I have to agree with that woman. I, too, have gained hope and strength from the MENtors group. The walk is an event I always look forward to. It is truly a remarkable sight to see such an eclectic group of men and boys walking together in high-heeled shoes. The age range must be somewhere between six and eighty years old, and they all have their own stories and reasons for coming. They all do it differently. Some strut, some stumble, and some drag their feet and pieces of their mangled shoes behind them. I truly feel they are a little different after participating. I know I am.

CHAPTER SEVENTEEN
Hope

"Only in the darkness can you see the stars."

—Martin Luther King Jr.

"*You* have a tattoo?"

"Yes, a Superman tattoo on my left shoulder."

"Can I see it?"

This is an exchange I've had with thousands of students in countless schools over the past ten years. I often share this little tidbit of information to build rapport with the groups and classes I work in. The response is always one of shock and awe as they realize I may not be the tea-toting, Shakespeare-reading old man they thought I was. There's usually a standard series of follow-up questions that come next.

"Did it hurt?"

"Did it bleed a lot?"

"How old were you when you got it?"

"Will you get another one?"

"Do your parents know you have it?"

"Were you drunk when you got it?" (This is *usually* reserved for inquisitive high school students.)

I wait patiently as the students shout out the questions, and I answer them the best I can. I'm waiting for a particular question that invariably will come up at some point in some form or another.

"Are you happy you got it?"

"Why did you choose Superman?"

"What does it mean to you?" (This is usually those high school students again.)

These are my opening. The answer to this last set of questions has changed a lot over the years, just as I have. At the start of my career in VAW work, the answers were simple. I liked comic books, with Superman being my favorite. I loved the idea of being invincible (yeah, I know about the kryptonite thing) and using powers to help people. During my early years, this answer would lead to some interesting conversation about what powers the students would want to have and how they would use them.

However, as the years have passed, I've realized this little tattoo has come to mean something else entirely. It's no longer about a cartoon figure flying in tights and a cape while keeping that perfect hair in place. It's become about the people I have met in my travels as a man working in the world of violence against women. Many of them have been children, but I would be remiss if I didn't include the extraordinary women and kind, compassionate men I have encountered. These people I have been lucky enough to meet have become the heroes of my story. They are the ones who have the courage to face another day after the last one was so difficult. They have the insight and humility to take a real look at who they are and who they want to be. They have found the power to change the course of their lives even when faced with what seems like insurmountable obstacles. The stories I've told in this recollection are about those people. The ones who don't need heat-ray vision or super speed to truly make change a reality. Some of the stories have been funny, some have been heartbreaking, and some truly remind me about the hope every person can carry with them every single day.

It's the story of the young boy who lives in a shelter with his mom but still gleefully sprints around in high heels. It's the teenage girl who was assaulted at a party who has the courage to get help. It's the dad who decides to pose with his daughter in a poster to promote a life free of violence for his—and everyone else's—daughter. It's the mom who makes the choice to leave home in the middle of the night so her children are safe. It's the young man who would spend all the money in the world just to have a healthy relationship with someone he loves. These faces and stories have become permanently engrained in my memory and have truly changed my life. Each one of those stories has given me hope and fueled my desire to see as many people as I can. I hope the programs I run with people can make a difference in their lives. I know their presence in my life has made a difference in mine.

Oh, by the way, I still do enjoy Superman stories. I've just come to realize true heroes walk amongst us every day.

CHAPTER EIGHTEEN
Current Day

"An education is not a thing that one gets, but a lifelong process."

—Gloria Steinem

A lot of my journey in a woman's shoes has been about hope. The hope I have seen in the eyes of the kids I've worked with, and the hope I get from seeing such courageous and amazing acts of compassion and kindness. But every now and then, it has been difficult to feel and remain hopeful.

In the autumn of 2016, I found myself feeling hopeless. It was on November 9, 2016, to be exact. This was the day the U.S. Presidential election results were announced. I had spent most of the days and weeks leading up to the election varying between feelings of horror, amusement, bewilderment and sickness at what was being said south of the border. But I, like most people, didn't for a second believe Donald Trump would actually become President of the United States. As we all learned, the seemingly impossible did occur.

On the morning of November 9th, I found myself driving to a local school, feeling shocked and confused by what had just occurred. I was going to the school to run my weekly boys group, and I wondered if the election results would be brought up by any of the guys. The election campaign had certainly been a topic of conversation amongst the students I had worked with over the last few months. I heard them talking about it during their nutrition breaks and was deeply concerned by what was said. Donald Trump had become a sort of cult hero to some of the guys. They seemed to take great pleasure in quoting some of his more outrageous statements. I looked forward to him being defeated and leaving the spotlight for a while. I also looked forward to not having to address the comments and opinions expressed in the campaign and repeated by so many students. But that was not to be.

Once I arrived at the school and began setting up for my group, the day started to feel normal. As so often happened, the distraction and regular routine made me forget about the bigger world issues. It wasn't too long into my setup that a teacher I greatly respected and had worked with for many years approached me. He seemed visibly upset. He quietly pulled me aside.

"So what are you going to tell the kids now?"

He didn't need to elaborate or explain because I knew what he meant. How could I extoll the virtues of respect, equality, and kindness after someone had just been rewarded on a platform that went against all those things? The truth was, I didn't have an answer. I felt hopeless and deeply discouraged, and things didn't improve once the group started.

If I were to be honest, the group was a gong show. The guys behaved worse than they had at any point before. It may have been a coincidence, and it may have been due to my mood, but it felt like they had received permission to act out.

I went home feeling pretty low that day. It was impossible to stop thinking about the election results because it was all anyone talked about. It was also difficult to answer the question I had been asked because I honestly didn't know how to make sense of things myself. How could I explain it to my students?

As fortune would have it, something happened that night that gave me a little more clarity. I was doing some work and was on my organization's website when a new post was added. It was the results for a local event held annually as a fundraiser for my organization. The event was organized and run each year by a husband and wife who had lost their daughter during a domestic dispute several years before. Tragically, their daughter's estranged husband had murdered her and then taken his own life. They had left behind two children as well as many family and friends. This event was held in memory of the daughter and was always an inspiring fundraiser for our organization. It had just been announced they had added to their yearly total of fundraised dollars and had now eclipsed the $75,000 mark. As I sat there looking and smiling at the pictures and messages posted from the event, I reflected on my day and the question asked of me earlier.

"So what are you going to tell the kids now?"

It suddenly seemed pretty simple. The parents I was looking at on my organization's website had been through the most difficult thing any parent would ever have to go through. They had lost their child in a violent and horrific way. But what did they do about it? They turned it into something positive and tried to make a difference. That was my answer, and when I was at the school the next week, I shared it with that teacher.

"We can't always stop bad things from happening. Sometimes we don't understand them, and they may never make sense. But when something bad does happen, the good people keep trying to make a difference."

The teacher stopped for a second and thought about my answer. He slowly smiled and said, "I figured you'd know what to say. I'm going to use that."

I began in my role as the only man working in a VAW organization over a decade ago. I didn't know at the time what a unique opportunity that was, and I had no idea what was in store for me. At the time, it was a job, plain and simple. It promised to be a good job, but it was still just a job. I was excited by the opportunity and for the chance it would give me to spend more time with my family.

I couldn't possibly have known when I started on December 16, 2006, my life would never be the same. I didn't have any premonition I would become an irrevocably different person, but that's what has happened. As I reflect on my first weeks and months on the job, I laugh at what I thought I knew. When I had answered interview questions about violence against women, I believed I understood the issue. I had so much to learn, and now I realize I still do.

I often think back to my old friend Phyllis. She had asked me a question all those years ago, and I have been wrestling with it ever since.

"So … are you a feminist?"

My answer then was one of self-defense. It was about saying something that sounded reasonable while trying to hide the fact I really didn't understand the question. But I think I understand the question now. It's less about "are you a feminist?" and more about "what do you believe?" I'm sorry, Phyllis, if I'm putting words in your mouth.

So what *do* I believe, and does that make me a feminist?

Well, here's what I believe. I believe in equality. I believe male privilege *does* exist. I believe I can help make a difference. Based on the simplest definition of "feminism," I am, in fact, a feminist. But what would people say if I rejected that term? Would it make what I believe less important or valid? I don't believe so. For me, it's less about what I am, more about what I believe, and most importantly, about how I behave. Luckily for me, what I believe and what I strive to be does align with feminism, and I'm proud to acknowledge that. As one of the men in my men's engagement group once said, "I had to become a feminist to become a better man."

That sums it up for me nicely.

EPILOGUE

It is the summer of 2019. It has been almost thirteen years since I began my journey in a woman's shoes. My daughter Katie is now fifteen years old and has grown into a strong, inspiring, and independent young woman. I know my time working in the field of violence against women has helped shape who she is today, and I'm very grateful for that. I feel I always would have been a good father, but my newfound work experiences increased what I was able to give Katie exponentially.

MENtors is no more. Due to a wide range of reasons, the men's group I helped start and was a part of for many years is no longer operating. I still see many of the men from the group around the community, and we often talk about the what we did and what still needs to be done. The legacy of men becoming more aware of the issue of violence against women was accomplished, albeit on a smaller scale than many of us had hoped for. But perhaps that's how it all begins, with a small group of people determined to make a difference.

For now, I remain the only male employee of my organization. It's still pointed out to me from time to time, in small and funny ways. Recently, one of the managers was talking about a work-related issue and said to all the staff, “It is time we all put on our big girl pants.” Everyone laughed and looked at me. I responded with, “I have no problem wearing the big girl pants (although, the lack of a fly would be irritating).”

I remain committed to what I do and to the young people I get to work with and help each day. It’s nice to reflect on where I started compared to where I am today. When I began my journey, I wanted a job that was important and made a difference. I wanted to be able to say that’s why I went to work each day. Today, I can say without any hesitation that I have that, and I look forward to doing it again tomorrow.

PHOTO ALBUM

Just before we strap on the shoes for our big walk
Photo by: Stacey Tarrant

Standing with my daughter Katie before the MENtors "Walk in Her Shoes"
Photo by Sabina Iurillo

The MENtors got to hang out with our local professional basketball team.
Photo by: Carissa Cooper

Proud to pose with The MENtors
Photo by Stacey Tarrant

Katie got to see her Dad and Papa walk in support of her right to a violence free future
Photo by: Sabina Iurillo

Remembering the lives we lost on December 6th.
Photo by: Stacey Tarrant

Promoting the high heeled shoe walk
Photo by Stacey Tarrant

The caption on the picture explains why I do the work I do each day. I wish that for Katie and every other daughter in the world too.
Photo by: Darryn Stevenson

ACKNOWLEDGMENTS

Before I started the process of writing a book, I was always slightly confused by the length of the acknowledgment page for most authors. After writing a book and bringing it to publication, I now understand why those acknowledgments are so lengthy. While the story in this book is mine, the book itself belongs to so many people who helped make it possible.

Neta Gear and Sue Buckle took a chance on a naïve and inexperienced guy almost fifteen years ago. The result of that gamble is this story. I can't express how thankful I am. I'd also like to recognize my current FTP team. Norah Kennedy and Lynette Pole-Langdon have supported me when it was easy and when it wasn't. Thank-you for believing in me. I am humbled and honored to call the staff at FTP my colleagues and friends. They truly do the difficult work at FTP, and as a result, the lives of so many children, women, and men are better.

I've had the opportunity to work with some very talented and inspiring educators. From the amazing teachers and administrators in my local schools to my fellow educators at FTP. These people work to help young people become the best versions of themselves. I'm proud to work alongside them.

The process of changing this book from my notes on a page to something people may want to invest their time in is due in part to many talented individuals.

Tiffany Fox at Beyond DEF Publishing Services made the process easy to understand and improved the quality of my work immensely. I can't imagine doing this project with anyone else.

Published author Allison Cosgrove patiently answered any questions I had and always pointed me in the right direction. Thank you for giving your time so generously.

Nancy Frater, owner of the local independent bookstore (Book Lore), helped to bring attention to my book and enthusiastically stood in my corner from day one. She is a reminder of why the independent local bookstores have been, and should continue to be, the lifeblood of every community.

Thank you to my initial editors. Tabi Wells took the time to give my book an excellent overhaul and helped give me the confidence to move forward. Andrea Stewart was the first person to read this book and has long been an inspirational and beloved friend.

The appreciation and gratitude I have for my family goes beyond words, but I'll try to express it as well as I can.

To my parents Christine, Dennis and Melody: thank you for showing me what it meant to be a respectful and caring man.

I'd also like to thank my siblings Shannon, Matt, and Laura. I spent different times in my life with each of you, and each of those time periods helped me become who I was meant to be. I'm extremely proud to be your brother.

Finally, to the inspirations for this journey.

To my daughter Katie: you have changed my life in ways I can never describe. You are the reason I do the work I do. Watching you grow up has been the joy of my life. I'm so proud of who you have become.

To my partner in life Sabina: everything I accomplish, I owe to you. You push me to be the best version of myself, and you love and accept me even when I fall short of that. No one could ask for more than the life you have given me.

Finally, to the women and children who have sought refuge at FTP over the years: your courage and resiliency has inspired me. I cannot express how deeply and sincerely I admire your strength.